PHILOSOPHY OF EDUCATION

DR. SAVITA MISHRA

Contents

Preface

Philosophy has its own methodology which cope up with its problems and nature. Philosophy gave us the origin of problems. It deals with the basic assumptions of the world of atomic propositions. It is to philosophize things to reach to its ultimate reality, truth and goal. It also leads its development in the field of mathematics, physics and humanities. The progress of philosophy is the progress of science. According to Plato, philosophy find it's origin in wonder or curiosity created in the mind of an individual.

This book 'Philosophy of Education' is very useful for students studying in B.Ed, M.Ed, B.A (Education), M.A (Education) and preparing for NET, SET and other competitive exams. This book fulfills all essential requirements and its wide circulation will definitely exert an important influence on the theory of Education. This book discusses about the Philosophy of Education such as concept of Samkhya, Vedanta, Nyaya,Yoga, Indian Philosophy and Heterodox of Indian Schools of Philosophy with special reference to the concept of knowledge, reality and values and their educational implications for aims, curriculum and method of education, Western Schools of Philosophy such as Idealism, Naturalism, Realism, Pragmatism and Scientific tendency in Education etc. for the benefit of mankind in general. Education has been immensely influenced by the educational ideas of such great personalities such as Ravindra Nath Tagore, Mahatma Gandhi, Aurobindo Ghosh, Swami Vivekananda etc. who have also given wisdom for guidance in the field of education. In this book, an attempt has been made to discuss the educational ideas of these great educators.

Dr Savita Mishra

CHAPTER ONE

MODERN CONCEPT OF PHILOSOPHY

Introduction

Modern philosophy is a branch of philosophy associated with the idea of modernity that originated during the modern era. Although much of it shares certain conclusions, which helps to distinguish it from earlier thinking, it is not a single theory or school (and thus should not be confused with Modernism). The 17th and early 20th centuries were loosely described as the beginning and end of modern thought. It's debatable how much of the Renaissance can be included, as well as whether modernity came to an end in the twentieth century, and was replaced by postmodernity. How you respond to these questions will decide how much you use the phrase "modern theory."

Modern Western Philosophy

It's debatable how much of the Renaissance philosophical tradition has made its way into modern philosophy. The Early Renaissance is often considered to be less modern and more mediaeval than the later High Renaissance. By the 17th and 18th centuries, the main figures of mind theory, epistemology, and metaphysics had been loosely divided into two groups. According to the "Rationalists," who were mostly from France and Germany, all understanding must begin with those "innate ideas" in the mind. Significant rationalists included Descartes, Baruch Spinoza, Gottfried Leibniz, and Nicolas Malebranche.

The "Empiricists," on the other hand, believed that perception began with sensory experience. Major figures in this school of thought include John Locke, George Berkeley, and David Hume (These are retrospective categories, for which Kant is largely responsible). Despite the fact that each of these thinkers worked on ethics in their own distinct ways, ethics and political theory are rarely included in these categories. Other notable political theorists include Thomas Hobbes and Jean-Jacques Rousseau.

In the late eighteenth century, Immanuel Kant introduced a groundbreaking philosophical system that sought to combine rationalism and empiricism. He did not completely settle the philosophical controversy, whether or not he was right. Kant sparked a whirlwind of academic activity in Germany in the early nineteenth century, beginning with German idealism. The defining theme of idealism was that the universe and the mind must be understood in terms of the same categories; this led to Georg Wilhelm Friedrich Hegel's work, which argued, among other things, that "the real is rational; the rational is real."

Renaissance Philosophy

In Renaissance humanism, which rejected dogma and scholasticism, the importance of human beings was emphasised (see Oration on the Dignity of Man). A new interest in human activities was sparked by Niccolavelli's The Prince, which aided the advancement of political science. Humanists were distinct from Medieval scholars in that they saw the natural world as mathematically organised and pluralistic rather than in terms of goals and objectives.

Rationalism

"I think, therefore I am," as René Descartes put it, is the standard starting point for modern philosophy. Scholasticism dominated philosophy in the early seventeenth century, founded on Plato, Aristotle, and early Church writings and written by theologians. According to Descartes, many of the prevalent Scholastic philosophical ideas are obsolete or incorrect. In other terms, he advocated starting theory from the beginning. He makes six brief essays in his most important work, Meditations on First Philosophy, that aim to do just that. He is attempting to set aside as many of his beliefs as possible in order to determine what, if anything, he knows for certain. He learns that he can doubt almost everything, including the nature of physical objects, God, his memory, history, science, and even mathematics, but he can't doubt that he's doubting at all. Even though it's not true, he knows what he's thinking about, and he's thinking about it right now. On this basis, he rebuilds his awareness. He realises that some of his feelings may not have come from him alone, but from God alone, and he proves God's presence. He then demonstrates that God would not be deceived in any way; in other words, he defends conventional science and reasoning approaches as fallible but not false.

Empiricism

Empiricism is a theory of science that opposes, among other things, rationalism, idealism, and historicism. Empiricism contends that knowledge comes (only or primarily) from sensory experience, in contrast to rationalism, which insists that knowledge comes (also) from pure thought. Empiricism and rationalism are individualist philosophies of interpretation, whereas historicism is a social epistemology. Historicism differs from empiricism in that it argues that sensory data cannot be perceived without taking into account the historical and cultural contexts in which they are created. Empiricism and empirical study should not be confused because they are contrasting opinions about how to best perform studies, and there is widespread consensus among researchers that studies should be observational. Empiricism is now recognised as one of the competing principles for gaining information and performing research. As a consequence, the concept of letting observational evidence "speak for themselves" is central to empiricism, although opposing views contradict this ideal. As a result, the term empiricism cannot be understood exclusively in terms of how it has been used in philosophical tradition.

It should also be constructed in a way that distinguishes empiricism from other epistemological positions in contemporary science and scholarship. In other words, in order to make meaningful distinctions between different ideals underlying contemporary science, empiricism as a theory must be formulated in accordance with other philosophies.

One of the opposing viewpoints that dominates epistemology, the study of human intelligence, is empiricism. Empiricism emphasises the role of experience and facts, especially sensory perception, in the development of ideas over the notion of inherent ideas or tradition, in contrast to rationalism, which relies on reason and may incorporate intuitive knowledge.

Idealism

Idealism is a metaphysical school of thought that claims life, or truth as we know it, is merely a mental construct or otherwise immaterial. Idealism is epistemologically expressed as scepticism regarding the possibility of comprehending any mind-independent matter. In a sociological sense, idealism emphasises how human ideas, especially beliefs and values, shape society. (nine) As an ontological philosophy, idealism goes even further, asserting that all things are made up of mind or spirit.

Analytic philosophy

Analytic theory influenced English-speaking countries in the twentieth century. In the United States, the United Kingdom, Canada, Scandinavia, Australia, and New Zealand, the vast majority of university philosophy departments are classified as "analytic." The term refers to a broad philosophical tradition marked by an emphasis on clarification and argument (often achieved through modern formal logic and language analysis), as well as a respect for natural sciences.

Historical Overview

Wisdom, philosophical culture and the pursuit of reality in a general sense are all synonyms for philosophy. All cultures and literate societies pose philosophical questions like "how are we to live" and "what is the nature of reality" in this sense. A broad and impartial understanding of philosophy finds a logical inquiry into such matters as reality, morality, and life in all world cultures.

Western Philosophy

Western philosophy is the intellectual tradition of the Western world, dating back to pre-Socratic thinkers such as Thales and Pythagoras, who were known as 'students of nature' and practised a 'love of knowledge' (Latin: philosophia).

There are three periods of Western philosophy:

* Ancient (Greco- Roman)
* Medieval Philosophy (referring to the Christian European thoughts)
* Modern Philosophy (beginning in the 17th century)

Ancient era

We know very little about the philosophers who came before Socrates, despite the fact that our knowledge of the ancient world begins with Thales in the 6th century BCE (commonly known as the pre-Socratics). The ancient world was ruled by Greek intellectual schools. Plato founded the Platonic Academy, and his pupil Aristotle founded the Peripatetic school, both of which were influenced by Socrates' teachings. Cynicism, Cyrenaicism, Stoicism, and Academic Skepticism were all influenced by Socrates.

Democritus, a contemporary of Socrates, influenced two other schools of thought: Pyrrhonism and Epicureanism. The Greeks were interested in metaphysics (with opposing ideas such as atomism and monism), cosmology, the essence of a happy existence (eudaimonia), the probability of knowledge, and the nature of reason (logos). Romans such as Cicero and Seneca began to address Greek philosophy in Latin with the rise of the Roman empire (see Roman philosophy).

Medieval era

Mediaeval philosophy (5th–16th centuries) refers to the period following the fall of the Western Roman Empire, which was dominated by the rise of Christianity and thus reflects Judeo-Christian theological concerns while maintaining continuity with Greco-Roman thought. Issues like God's life and purpose, the nature of faith and reason, metaphysics, and the problem of evil were all discussed during this time. Some of the most influential Medieval thinkers include St. Augustine, Thomas Aquinas, Boethius, Anselm, and Roger Bacon. Because these thinkers saw philosophy as an ancilla theologiae (addition to theology), they tried to match their philosophy to their interpretation of sacred scripture. Scholasticism flourished during this time period, a text critical method developed in mediaeval universities that focused on close reading and debate on key texts. There was a greater emphasis on classic Greco-Roman thought and a strong Humanism during the Renaissance.

Modern era

Early modern thought in the Western world begins with thinkers like Thomas Hobbes and René Descartes. After the advent of natural science, modern philosophy was concerned with establishing a secular and logical basis for knowledge, moving away from traditional systems of authority such as faith, scholastic thinking, and the Church. Some of the most influential modern philosophers include Spinoza, Leibniz, Locke, Berkeley, Hume, and Kant.

The Enlightenment, which included figures such as Hegel, a crucial role in German idealism, Kierkegaard, who built the grounds for existentialism, Nietzsche, a famous anti-Christian, John Stuart Mill, who supported utilitarianism, and Karl Marx, who built the foundations for communism, influenced 19th-century philosophy. The twentieth century saw the split between analytic and continental philosophy, as well as philosophical movements such as phenomenology, existentialism, logical positivism, pragmatism, and the linguistic turn (see Contemporary philosophy).

Middle Eastern Philosophy

Pre-Islamic Philosophy

The earliest known philosophical wisdom literature can be found in the Fertile Crescent, Iran, and Arabia, and Islamic culture now dominates the region. Wisdom Literature was a genre that used stories and proverbs to teach people about ethical behaviour, practical life, and morality in the early Fertile Crescent. These texts, known in Ancient Egypt as sebayt ('teachings,') are crucial to our understanding of Egyptian philosophy. Many metaphysical cosmological speculations in Babylonian astronomy may have influenced the Ancient Greeks.

Both Jewish and Christian philosophy have their roots in the Middle East and Europe, and they share monotheistic beliefs and some early Judaic texts (primarily the Tanakh). Greek and Islamic philosophy piqued the interest of Jewish thinkers such as the Geonim of the Babylonian Talmudic Academies and Maimonides. Moses Mendelssohn's works, which helped to usher in the Haskalah (Jewish Enlightenment), Jewish existentialism, and Reform Judaism, are examples of later Jewish thought influenced by strong Western intellectual influences. The numerous practices of Gnosticism emerged in the first century, inspired by both Greek and Abrahamic currents and focusing on spiritual insight (gnosis).

Islamic Philosophy

Islamic philosophy is a branch of philosophy that has its roots in the Islamic tradition and is conducted primarily in Arabic. It is influenced by both Islamic and Greco-Roman thought. The translation movement (mid-eighth to late-tenth century) culminated in the Arabic translation of Greek philosophical works following the Muslim conquests. In a modern and creative way, early Islamic philosophy advanced Greek intellectual traditions. The Islamic Golden Age began with this academic achievement. The two main currents of early Islamic thought are Kalam, which focuses on Islamic theology, and Falsafa, which focuses on Aristotelianism and Neoplatonism.

Aristotle's work inspired philosophers such as Al-Kindi, Avicenna, and Averroes. Others, such as Al-Ghazali, were harsh opponents of the Islamic Aristotelians' methods and thought their theological theories were heretical. For example, Ibn al-Haytham and Al-Biruni created a scientific method, experimental medicine, an optics theory, and a legal philosophy.

Islamic thought influenced European intellectual developments significantly, especially through Averroes' Aristotelian commentaries. The fall of Baghdad and the Mongol invasions of 1258 are generally regarded as the end of the Golden Age. Many schools of Islamic philosophy flourished after the Golden Age, including Illuminationist philosophy, Sufi philosophy, and Transcendent theosophy. In the 19th and 20th centuries, the Nahda movement (literally "Awakening"; also known as the "Arab Renaissance") inspired contemporary Islamic thought in the Arab world.

Indian Philosophy

The various philosophical traditions that have evolved on the Indian subcontinent since ancient times are referred to as Indian philosophy (Sanskrit: darana, lit. 'perspective'). Indian philosophical traditions share a number of central concepts and ideas, which are represented in a variety of ways and accepted or rejected by different traditions. These principles include dhárma, karma, prama, dukha, sasra, and moka. The Upanishads of the later Vedic period are among the oldest surviving Indian philosophical texts, and are thought to preserve Brahmanism's ideas. The relationship between Indian philosophy and the Vedas, as well as the ideas contained within them, is commonly used to categorise it. After the Vedic period, Hinduism's various traditions largely arose as separate traditions, while Jainism and Buddhism appeared at the end of the Vedic period.

Hindus classify Indian philosophical traditions as either orthodox (stika) or heterodox (nstika), depending on whether they acknowledge the Vedas' authority and the brahman and tman doctrines found within them. Hindu philosophers of the six orthodox schools developed systems of epistemology (pramana) and studied topics such as metaphysics, ethics, psychology (gua), hermeneutics, and soteriology within the sense of Vedic wisdom, while providing a wide range of interpretations. The six orthodox schools were the competing religious practices in what has been called the "Hindu synthesis" of classical Hinduism.

East Asian Philosophy

The "Hundred Schools of Thought" flourished during the Western Zhou Dynasty and the following periods after its decline, and East Asian philosophical thought started in Ancient China. During this period, China's major philosophical schools, such as Confucianism (also known as Ruism), Legalism, and Taoism, as well as numerous other less prominent schools like Mohism and Naturalism, experienced significant intellectual and cultural developments. Tao, Yin and yang, Ren and Li are examples of metaphysical, political, and ethical theories established by these philosophical traditions. During the Han and Tang periods, these schools of thought evolved further, resulting in new philosophical movements such as Xuanxue (also known as Neo-Taoism) and Neo-Confucianism. Neo-Confucianism was a syncretic philosophy that blended ideas from various Chinese philosophical traditions, such as Buddhism and Taoism. During the Song dynasty, Neo-Confucianism came to dominate the educational system, and its theories served as the intellectual foundation for imperial exams for the scholar official class.

The Tang scholars Han Yu and Li Ao, as well as the Song thinkers Zhou Dunyi and Zhu Xi, are among the most prominent Neo-Confucian thinkers. The Confucian canon, which consists of the Four Books, was compiled by Zhu Xi (the Great Learning, the Doctrine of the Mean, the Analects of Confucius, and the Mencius). Wang Yangming, a Ming scholar, is a later but significant philosopher in this tradition.

Buddhism first arrived in China during the Han Dynasty, through the Silk Road, and developed distinct Chinese forms (such as Chan/Zen) that spread across the East Asian cultural sphere due to native influences.

Chinese culture had a major impact on the cultures of other East Asian countries, and Chinese philosophy had a strong impact on Korean, Vietnamese, and Japanese philosophy. A later Chinese dynasties, such as the Ming Dynast and the Korean Joseon dynasty, saw a resurgent Neo-Confucianism, led by thinkers like Wang Yangming, emerge as the dominant school of thought, supported by the imperial state. Confucian philosophy inspired the Tokugawa shogunat in Japan as well. A confucianism continues to have an impact on the ideas and worldviews of Chinese cultural nations today.

Chinese thinkers adapted concepts from Western thought throughout the Modern period. Mao Zedong influenced the development of Chinese Marxist ideology, while Hu Shih influenced the development of Chinese pragmatism. In the twentieth century, old conservative ideologies began to reassert themselves. New Confucianism, for example, has grown in popularity thanks to figures like Xiong Shili. Humanistic Buddhism, on the other hand, is a relatively new modernist Buddhist movement. In the meantime, strong Western influences influenced early Japanese thinking, such as the study of Western Sciences (Rangaku) and the modernist Meirokusha intellectual culture, which drew on European enlightenment thought and advocated political changes as well as Western philosophies such as Liberalism and Utilitarianism. The "National Studies" (Kokugaku) tradition was another modern Japanese philosophical movement. This academic movement aimed to research and encourage ancient Japanese culture and thought. Kokugaku thinkers like Motoori Norinaga aspired to return to a pure Japanese culture known as Shinto, which they saw as free of foreign influences.

Branches of Philosophy

Philosophical issues can be divided into many categories. These divisions allow philosophers to concentrate on a collection of related topics and engage with other thinkers who share their interests. These divisions aren't exhaustive, and they're still not mutually exclusive. (A philosopher could focus on Kantian epistemology, Platonic aesthetics, or contemporary political philosophy.) Furthermore, these philosophical inquiries often intersect with one another as well as with other fields of study such as science, religion, and mathematics.

Aesthetics

"Critical reflection on art, culture, and nature" is a definition of aesthetics. It deals with the development and appreciation of beauty, as well as the essence of art, beauty and taste, enjoyment, emotional values, and perception. It's more specifically defined as the analysis of sensory or sensori-emotional values, also known as sentiment and taste judgments. Art theory, literary theory, film theory, and music theory are the four main divisions. Determining the collection of values underlying the work of a specific artist or artistic movement, such as the Cubist aesthetic, is an example of art theory.

Ethics

Ethics, or moral philosophy, is the study of what constitutes good and bad behaviour, right and wrong principles, and good and evil. Its main topics of investigation are how to live a healthy life and how to define moral values. It also entails determining whether there is a better way to live or a universal moral principle, and, if so, how we think about it. Normative ethics, meta-ethics, and applied ethics are the three major divisions of ethics. The following are the three major ethical viewpoints about what constitutes moral behaviour:

- Consequentialism is a theory that measures decisions based on their outcomes. Utilitarianism is one such viewpoint, which evaluates behaviour based on their net happiness (or pleasure) and/or lack of misery (or pain).
- Deontology is the study of whether or not one's acts are in line with one's moral obligations. Deontology, in the standard form defended by Immanuel Kant, is concerned with whether a decision, regardless of its implications, honours the moral agency of other people.
- Virtue ethics is a branch of ethics that evaluates acts based on the moral character of the person doing them and whether they are consistent with

what an ideal virtuous person would do.

Other sub-fields: Mind Language

The study of language's meaning, origins, and use is known as linguistic philosophy. The essence of the mind and its relationship to the body is explored in philosophy of mind, which is typified by debates between materialism and dualism. This division has recently been linked to cognitive science.

Philosophy of Science

The foundations, methods, history, consequences, and intent of science are all investigated in science philosophy. Many of its subdivisions refer to different scientific fields. Philosophy of biology, for example, focuses on the philosophical, epistemological, and ethical questions that arise in the biomedical and life sciences.

Political Philosophy

The analysis of government and the relationship of individuals (or families and clans) to societies, including the state, is known as political philosophy. [requires citation] It covers topics such as justice, law, land, and citizen rights and responsibilities. Political philosophy, ethics, and aesthetics have all been lumped together under the umbrella of value theory because they all have a normative or evaluative component.

Applied and Professional Philosophy

Professional philosophers are those who study philosophy and work as professors in academic schools, teaching, researching, and writing. [No. 98] Most students of academic philosophy, on the other hand, go on to work in law, journalism, religion, research, politics, business, or the arts. Comedians Steve Martin and Ricky Gervais, filmmaker Terrence Malick, Pope John Paul II, Wikipedia co-founder Larry Sanger, technology pioneer Peter Thiel, Supreme Court Justice Stephen Bryer, and Vice Presidential nominee Carly Fiorina are only a few of the public figures with philosophy degrees. Philosophical tools, according to Curtis White, are important in the humanities, sciences, and social sciences.

The million-dollar Berggruen Prize, first awarded to Charles Taylor in 2016, is one of the most recent attempts to bring philosophers' work and importance to the general public. Some philosophers contend that the discipline has suffered as a result of this professionalisation.

Conclusion

Philosophy is the systematic analysis of concepts and problems, the rational exploration of universal values, the search for a holistic view of the universe, the study of ethical standards, and much more. Every aspect of human experience poses concerns that its strategies and hypotheses can answer, and its methods can be applied to any topic or vocation. Philosophy is, in certain ways, unavoidable: any thoughtful individual is confronted with philosophical problems, and nearly everyone is motivated by philosophical assumptions, even if unconsciously. It is not necessary to be unprepared. To a large degree, one can choose how reflective one will be in clarifying and forming one's philosophical conclusions, as well as how well prepared one will be for the philosophical dilemmas that life will present. Philosophical experience improves our problem-solving capacity, as well as our ability to comprehend and articulate concepts and persuasion skills. It also fosters an appreciation for things that are lacking in many people's lives, such as aesthetic knowledge, contact with a variety of people, vibrant discussion of current events, discerning evaluation of human nature, and intellectual zeal. In these and other respects, philosophy contributes immeasurably to academic and non-academic endeavours.

The problem-solving, logical, judgmental, and synthesising capacities that philosophy fosters have no limits in terms of distance or utility. This makes philosophy an excellent training for positions of leadership, management, or duty. A major or minor in philosophy can be easily incorporated with the requirements for almost any entry-level job; however, philosophical training, particularly in the development of many transferable skills, is especially important for career advancement in the long run.

Any course of study cannot guarantee wisdom, leadership, or the ability to resolve human conflicts; however, philosophy has historically followed these principles systematically, and its techniques, literature, and theories are constantly used in the quest to realise them. Sound logic, logical thought, well-crafted writing, judgement sophistication, a deep sense of relevance, and enlightened consciousness are never outdated, and they are never subject to market-place fluctuations. The most direct, and in many cases the only, path to the full development of these qualities is to learn philosophy.

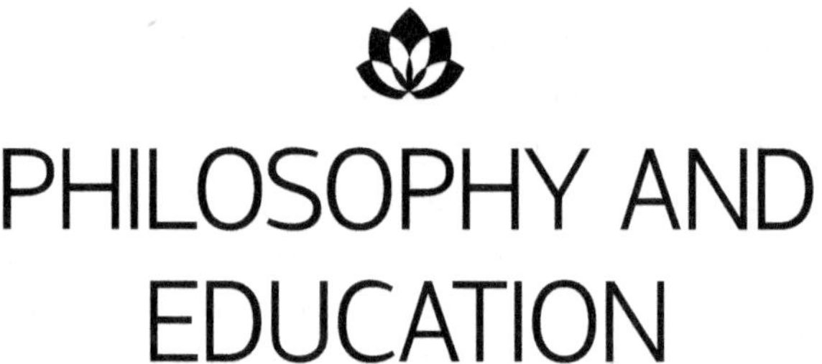

CHAPTER TWO

PHILOSOPHY AND EDUCATION

Introduction

Human endeavour is basically inquisitive, always absorbed in curiosity and exploration. Every human being in order to satisfy his needs runs almost in an aimless manner, which ends up sometimes satisfactorily and mostly in other time drives to dissatisfaction. We all are almost satisfied with ourselves for a small amount of time, otherwise most of the time we are in quest of satisfaction. The aimless endeavour of human beings needs a check. And in this field, it is only the study of philosophy that will bear fruits. In this regard for preparing human souls saturated with the knowledge that will help them to reach proper goals and ultimately establish them as good and responsible human beings and at the same time good citizens, the pathfinders are the teachers. The teachers are vested with the great responsibility to prepare good and powerful souls to run the society as a whole. In this regard, it is very much necessary for the teachers to study philosophy, to know why philosophy should be read, and how it could be implemented for preparing future generation.

Philosophy gives us more power to act and live. A true philosophy is an "esprite de ensemble", a synoptic vision of reality. It is the intellectual search for the fundamental truth of things. Philosophy deals with being as much as with becoming. The Philosopher is a lover of knowledge and never as a sole possessor of it. Every new filed of experience has its own laws. Human thought which always divides reality into form and essence, subject and object, 'that' and 'what', can never truly represent the reality which is an all inclusive spiritual unity. Philosophy can be an effort to dissolve again into the whole, the ocean of life which we are immersed, hence we draw the very force to labour and to live and from which both matter and intellect originate.The rationalists, in the early dawn of modern philosophy, defined metaphysics as a knowledge deduced from self-evident principles. This attempt at rationalization or mathematisation of philosophy sought to make it more exact. But metaphysics with thought as its instrument should never dream of being exact like mathematics since thought, though real cannot be identified with reality. Contemporary thought witnesses a chaos in the filed of metaphysics.

It is generally agreed by all that philosophy must be based on experience but often the term experience gets limited to certain specific regions.The work of philosophy is to arrange the data given by the various means of knowledge and put them into synthetic relation to the one truth.Philosophy should be all comprehensive, synthetic, affirmative and spiritual. Philosophy is the knowledge of ultimate reality. But ultimate reality, as Indian Philosophy truly maintains is not only existence but also consciousness. Thus philosophy as the quest after ultimate truth can also be defined as the science of value per excellence, which should not only criticize facts but also satisfy human aspirations.

A philosophy of education is an assertion (or set of statements) that identifies and explains the beliefs, values and understandings of an individual or group with respect to education. Defined in this sense, it may be thought of as a more-or-less organised body of knowledge and assessment on education, both as it is conceptualised and as it is drilled. To expound further, philosophy and education are the two flowers of one stem, the two different sides of one coin. One can never be considered without the other. The presence of one is fragmented without the other.The art of education cannot be completed without philosophy and philosophy cannot change others over to its points and qualities without education. There is a close interaction between the two; one without the other is unserviceable. Educational philosophy is the utilization of the various aspects of philosophy in education. Education is the best means for the proliferation of a Philosophy. John Adams says, "Education is the dynamic side of Philosophy". It is the dynamic part of philosophical belief, a practical means of realizing the ideals of life.

However, a close perception of the different interpretations of philosophy will prove that these two are only the one and same thing seen from different angles. Philosophy is the study of the real factors, the pursuit of wisdom.It is not mere theorizing yet something which falls into place without any issues for each person. An individual who dives deep into the explanation and nature of things and attempts to arrive at certain general principles with a view to apply them in his everyday life, is a philosopher.In a wider sense philosophy is a way of looking at life, nature and truth. It sets up the ideals for a person to accomplish them in his lifetime.

Meaning of Philosophy

The most simple answer to this question is that it is an academic discipline. However, Pierre Hadot argues that philosophy was originally meant to be a "way of life". If we agree to the fact that philosophy has ethics as one of its main fields then it is undeniable on our part that philosophy teaches us the way to live life. To study or to know about philosophy does not mean that one has started to live a reasonable or moral life. But of course, it imparts the sense that the individual has become more than ever reasonable, ethical or moral in his/her life.

Philosophy, therefore, must be taken and accepted on personal terms. It has become very much necessary to consider or know what should be our goal of life and what decisions to be taken to keep up a moral life, in spite of all kinds of situations in life. What major areas of our nature that we need to change with the assistance of philosophy are our thoughts, belief, and actions.

Thinking: Philosophy does not tell us what to believe. It helps us to think reasonably and to culture, positive believes. Only reading philosophy will not be enough. It needs to be put into practice. Philosophy when put into practice makes us reasonable. Reading, writing and debating philosophy helps improve our intuitive ability to understand what it means to be reasonable. Our thinking is influenced by how we think. Philosophy helps assure us that manipulation and poor arguments will have a lower impact on our beliefs and good arguments and evidence will have a larger impact on our beliefs. Being reasonable does not assure that what we believe is true, but at least it comforts us by making sure that our beliefs are better, or are more reasonable.

Beliefs: Philosophy asserts on us to question our own belief. It helps us to change our mind when we find out a belief we have is unjustified. The belief can be in any area whether ethical, political, or social and is open enough to be questioned. The change of belief raises our level of knowledge and makes us more absorbed and confident.

Actions: When we start to culture better beliefs, we are in a more confident position to improve our behaviour. When our actions get improved, we are more satisfied, calm and are able to process better and improved thoughts further for the generation ahead who are looking forward to us.

Importance of Philosophy

Philosophy contributes very crucially to the educational compass by its dictating demand upon intellectual activity. Education in philosophy means getting aware of the developments in the history of philosophy, learning the latest techniques, and answers to philosophical questions, and at the greater level learning critical, interpretative, and evaluative skills that play their role in the overall scheme of things. Philosophical methods can be applied in various fields and subjects. Whatever we learn in philosophy can be virtually applied in our many endeavours. The study of philosophy helps us to enhance our ability to solve problems, our communication skills, our persuasive powers, and our writing skills. Here is an attempt to point out how philosophy helps us develop these various important skills to sharpen the qualities existing within for the betterment of self as well a for the upcoming generation.

Skills of Problem Solving: With the study of philosophy, a person develops the ability of problem-solving. It helps us to analyse concepts, definitions, arguments and problems. It enhances the capacity to organize ideas and issues to deal with questions of value and to skim and scan from large quantities of information. The study of philosophy helps us to find out fine and subtle differences between views and also to uncover the common ground between opposing poles. It also helps us to synthesize a variety of views or perspective into one unified whole.

Persuasive Powers: It provides training in the construction of clear ideas, well-constructed arguments and appropriate examples. It enhances our ability to be more convincing to others. We develop an ability to defend our own views, to appreciate opposite views and at the same time to assert forcefully our own views as preferable to alternatives. All these capacities can be developed by the practice of philosophy not only within the classroom but also outside the classroom, where everything turns to be a part of philosophical education.

Communication Skills: A unique contribution of philosophy can be witnessed in the development of communicative powers. The study and gaining a clear perception in philosophy helps us to make smart use of self-expression tools, for instance, skill in the use of arguments with the use of well-formed ideas. It enhances our ability to explain satisfactorily what is difficult with the elimination of ambiguities and vagueness from our speech or even writing.

Writing Skills: Writing skill is developed by the inclusion of concrete examples, interpretative arguments, assertion or establishment of ideas.

Understanding Other Disciplines: Philosophy has an incredible contribution to enhance our ability to understand other disciplines. Many important questions about a discipline, such as the nature of its concepts and its relation to other disciplines, are philosophical in nature. Philosophy of science, for example, is needed to supplement the understanding of the natural and social sciences that derives from scientific works itself. Philosophy of literature and philosophy of history are of similar value in understanding the humanities, and philosophy of art (aesthetics) is important in understanding both the visual and the performing arts. Philosophy is moreover, essential in assessing the various standards of evidence used by other disciplines. Since all field of knowledge employ reasoning and must set standards of evidence, logic and epistemology have a general bearing on all these fields.

Development of Sound Methods of Research and Analysis: Another value of philosophy is in the research work. It helps to formulate a hypothesis, to do research. Accordingly, it helps to gather relevant data, formulate ideas and use objective methods for assessing ideas and proposals. It hopefully transforms our ideas into new directions for the formulation of a new hypothesis.

Thus we can see that the study of philosophy helps us in various ways and at the same time continuously enhances our existing nerves to keep bouncing with good and confident thoughts.

Concept of Philosophy

The term "Philosophy" is derived from a Greek word "philosophia" which means "love of wisdom". It refers to the search for wisdom, fact or truth and the relationship among ideas. The man who engages himself/ herself in this effort is known as Philosopher. Philosophy can also be defined as the study of the fundamental nature of knowledge, reality and existence as an academic discipline. The person who has the taste for every sort of knowledge and who is curious to learn and is never satisfied may be termed as philosopher.

A person undergoes lots of experiences in his/her life from birth to death coupled with variety of problems related to knowledge, reality and world. In order to solve these problems he/she evaluates over them rationally by utilising his/her experiences. All this exercises enhance individual's wisdom. In this way, every individual is a philosopher at his/her own level but technically philosophers are designated only to those people who can guide others by influencing their ideas and actions with their own.

According to Indian Philosophy, the concept of Philosophy or Darshan is a bit different. The term "Philosophy" has been derived from a sanskrit word "Dristi" which means "to see". This thought is not physical, it is rather metaphysical or intuitional in nature. It leads an individual to the realization of truth. Thus, truth is the direct realization of self. Intuition of self is nothing but liberation from the bond of this mundane life (Moksha). Thus, Darshan is actually contributive to achieve Moksha.

Definition of Philosophy

The term Philosophy referred to any body of knowledge and it is closely related to religion, mathematics, natural science, education and politics. Different philosophers have defined the term Philosophy according to their own mature thinking and reflection. The below mentioned definitions can make it more clear to understand philosophy:

Aristotle : "Philosophy is a science which investigates the nature of being, as it is in itself".

Bertrand Russell : "Philosophy like all other studies, aims primarily at knowledge".

Brightman : "Philosophy may be defined as the attempt to think truly about human experience as a whole and to make our whole experience intelligible".

Fichte : "Philosophy is the science of knowledge".

Harold Titus : "A person's philosophy is the sum of his fundamental belief and convictions".

Henderson : "Philosophy is a search for a comprehensive view of nature, an attempt at a universal explanation of the nature of things".

Kant : "Philosophy is the science and criticism of cognition".

Marcus Tullius Cisero : "Philosophy is the mother of all arts and the true medicine of mind".

Plato : "Philosophy aims at knowledge of eternal nature of things".

Prem Nath : "Philosophy is open mindedness cultivated through the rigorous discipline of mind".

Radhakrishnan : "Philosophy is a logical enquiry into the nature of reality".

Raymont : "Philosophy is an unceasing effort to discover the general truth that lies behind the particular facts, to discern also the reality that lies behind appearances".

V. R. Taneja : "Philosophy being a mother of discipline, all arts and sciences look to it for the solution of their problems".

It is clear that all the sciences that have taken birth so far originated into philosophy. Philosophy is the truth or wisdom gained out of human knowledge and experience as a consequence of his/her interaction with the unfolded facts of nature. Philosophy is a attempt to answer the ultimate questions of life. It is an attitude towards human life and universe where the effort is made to search for truth on the basis of logical enquiry. It determines not only direction of knowledge but it also establishes the aims of life/education in a particular society. Aims of education vary as much as there is variation in the individual and socio-political philosophy of the people. Philosophy is actually the base of all educational thoughts.

Nature of Philosophy

Philosophy has its own methodology which cope up with its problems and nature. Philosophy gave us the origin of problems. It deals with the basic assumptions of the world of atomic propositions. It is to philosophize things to reach to its ultimate reality, truth and goal. It also leads its development in the field of mathematics, physics and humanities. The progress of philosophy is the progress of science. According to Plato, philosophy find it's origin in wonder or curiosity created in the mind of an individual.

The nature of philosophy is totally based on thinking ability and thoughts of human mind and also the actual nature of philosophy is to present the total world-view of its problems. As the term philosophy is derived from two Greek words Philo and Sophia which means "the love of wisdom" when the ancient Greek thinkers referred to wisdom, they usually meant the knowledge of fundamental principles and laws, an awareness of that which was basic and consistent as opposed to those things that are transitory and changing.

The term philosophy and philosopher was coined by Pythagoras. Philosophy as we know is the study of wisdom i.e. knowledge of ultimate causes, explanations and principles of things and the one who loves this wisdom is called philosopher. Philosopher knows every problem from its root and interprets it through rational basis. Philosophy, the mother of all science is the foundation and the touchstone of every subject. According to the exponent of modern western philosophy, Descartes, philosophy is originated from the feeling of skepticism in the mind of an individual.

Human mind is restless, it is always active in search of reality or truth. When man faces difficulties in this world, he is shaken and he tries to find the ways and mean to solve these problems.

Philosophy aims at a rational conception of the reality as a whole. It seeks to gain true insight into the general structure of the universe and man's relation to it. It seeks to investigate the nature of matter, life, soul and God, and their interrelations of one another. Philosophy also finds its origin into religion. God would have never left the man without guidance when he was created. Thus, guided principles, what is wrong or right, what is proper or improper, what is hell or heaven and so on which can lead an individual to a right direction is philosophy.

Problems of Philosophy

Philosophical problems are mainly of two types. On one hand, there are problems of those studies which are known as philosophical sciences, which includes logic, metaphysics, philosophy of religion, philosophy of science etc. On the other hand, there are problems which fall within the field of philosophy as a universal science.

1.Problems of philosophical sciences: It includes the problems of the sciences which are different from physical sciences in spite of bearing the name science. The main difference between philosophical science and the physical science is that the former raise more fundamental and basic questions as compared to the latter. Other philosophical sciences raise fundamental problems in their own field. The main problems of philosophical sciences are as follows:Metaphysical problems, Epistemological problems, Logical problems, Problems of sementics, Axiological problems, Problems of aesthetics, Problems of philosophy of science, Ethical problems, Problems of philosophy of religion and Problems of philosophy of social sciences.

2.Problems of philosophy as a comprehensive science: Philosophy also acts as a comprehensive science, it's important problems are as follows: Criticism of different sciences which includes criticism of basic postulates of different sciences and criticism of the conclusion of different sciences, Synthesis of different sciences and Historical problems of the origin of sciences.

Scope of Philosophy

The scope of philosophy can be divided into following parts:

A.Field of philosophical sciences: It includes different philosophical sciences such as metaphysics, epistemology, logic, sementics, axiology, ethics, aesthetics, philosophy of sciences, philosophy of religion, philosophy of history, philosophy of education, economic philosophy etc. All these are the important parts of the field of philosophy.

B.Field of philosophy as a comprehensive science: Philosophy is the science of sciences, the mother of all sciences. It's scope includes the criticism and synthesis of the postulates and conclusions of the physical and social sciences.

C.Subject matter of philosophy: It clarifies its subject matter which includes the conclusions and postulates of all the physical and social sciences besides their general problems. The object of philosophy is to take over the results of the various sciences, and add them to the result of religious and ethical experiences of mankind reflects upon the whole, hoping to be able to reach some general conclusions.

Philosophy aims at a rational conception of the reality as a whole. It seeks to gain true insight into the general structure of the universe and man's relation to it. It seeks to investigate the nature of matter, life, soul and God, and their interrelations of one another.

Education is the basic human need, and essential for a decent living and moral life. Without education the human society would be uncivilized and useless hum grouping, without any social, political, religious, and physical developments. Before discussing the relationship between philosophy and education first we would understand and what is education and then philosophy. Principles and values of life learnt through education and experience gives birth to philosophy in one's life.Philosophy lays the foundation of leading one's life based on our principles. Education is the source of learning and philosophy it's applications in our daily life. Education and philosophy, the two disciplines, are very closely related and in some areas they overlap each other. It is quite often said that, 'Philosophy and Education are two sides of the same coin'. 'Education is the dynamic side of philosophy'.

To elaborate further, 'Philosophy and Education are the two flowers of one stem, the two sides of one coin. One can never be thought of without the other. The presence of one is incomplete without the other. The art of education cannot be completed without philosophy and philosophy cannot convert others to its aims and values without education. There is a close interaction between the two; one without the other is unserviceable.'

Definitions of Education

Education has been defined by various scholars according to their cultural and social set ups. The few definitions are as follows:

i) Swami Vivekananda- "Education is the manifestation of perfection already reached in man."

ii) Aristotle- "Education is the process through which a sound mind is developed in a sound body".

iii) Plato- "Education is to develop physically and mentally in a human being in such a way that his/her potentialities should be created. "

iv) Dewey- "Education is the process to develop all the capabilities of a person as he could control his environment. "

v) Al Ghazali says, education is the process to enable an individual to know between true and false, good and bad, and right and wrong conducts.

vi) AlMaududi says, education is the process to bring the potential good in a man.

Philosophy and Education

Education is the fundamental human need, and essential for a decent-respectable living and moral life. Without education the human society would be uncivilized futile murmur meeting, and useless hum grouping, without any social, political, religious, and physical developments. Before discussing the connection among philosophy and education first we would comprehend and what is education and afterward philosophy.

Scope ofPhilosophy in Education

The general scope of philosophy is tremendous. Within its scope, we discuss soul, God, mystic powers, the inception of the universe, its extension and development, truth, morality, aesthetics and rationale. The subject Philosophy can be divided into three major divisions – They are:I. Metaphysics, II. Epistemology and III. Axiology. These branches are especially significant in the various aspects of education ranging from curriculum construction to its transaction in the classroom.

1. **Metaphysics:** Metaphysics is that branch of philosophy, which deals with the nature of reality. Metaphysics attempts to respond to the inquiry,What is real? The purpose of education is to explain 'reality' to the students. Is there a purpose in life? Does life have a meaning? Is there a set of enduring principles that control the activity of the universe? etc. It was Aristotle who built up the study of Metaphysics.

2. **Epistemology:** Whereas metaphysics is concerned with the nature of reality, Epistemology focuses on our insight into this reality. Epistemology deals with the theory concerning the different aspects of knowledge and

its procurement. Epistemology attempts to answer, "How would we get knowledge? How does a man realize what is genuine? Knowledge is of different types – revealed knowledge, intuitive knowledge, empirical knowledge, rational knowledge and authoritative knowledge.

3. **Axiology:** Axiology is that part of Philosophy, which is concerned about values. It is an attempt to find and recommend principles for choosing what activities and qualities are generally beneficial and why they are so. Axiology has two significant subdivisions – Ethics and Aesthetics. Ethics is concerned with good and bad, right and wrong and approval and disapproval as well as virtue and vice. Aesthetics is inquiry into the nature of what is beautiful or ugly and why it is so. Axiology is the well spring of the aim of education. All education and all type of schooling are integrated with values of life. Consciously or unknowingly, teachers are agents of value development and transmission.

Relationship between Philosophy and Education

Philosophy and education are two different fields of studies but they are closely linked together, because without any rational thinking prior to education, the whole educational process is directionless. The relationship between philosophy and education is explained as follows:

i) Meaning: Education means modification of the child's native behaviour. But the problem is in which direction modification should be carried out and what should be the standards and values, to strive for. This problem is solved by philosophy which points out the way to be followed by the educator in the modification of the child's behaviour. Philosophy, thus, deals with the ends and education is a laboratory' in which philosophic theories and speculations are tested and made concrete. Education may, therefore, be rightly called applied philosophy. Philosophy is wisdom; education transmits that wisdom from one generation to the other. Philosophy is in reality the theory of education. In other words, education is the dynamic side of philosophy, or application of the fundamental principles of philosophy. Philosophy formulates the method, education its process. Philosophy gives ideals, values and principles. Education works out those ideals, values and principles.

ii) Aims & Objectives: Education in every society is directed for specific aims and objectives. That aims and objectives are set by a philosophical approach. For example the aims of Pakistani education are to develop socially and morally sound person on the principles of Islam. So our whole educational set up aim is the creation of that kind of person and that aim is set by Islamic Philosophy. If Plato wants an ideal state so he uses education as an instrument and set aims and objectives to be achieved by his ideal educational plan.

iii) Methods & Curriculum: Every educational system is based upon specific teaching methodologies and the curriculum. What should be the teaching methodology? And what kind of teacher should be? And what kind of curriculum be taught to the students? All the answers are given by philosophy. So education is dependent on philosophy for guidance in various of areas.

iv) Philosophy of Education: There is a separate branch of philosophy which is called philosophy of education. The branch investigates that what should be the nature of education? Whether the educational aims be based on specific religion, social, moral, scientific basis. And how these aims can be achieved?

v) Education is the Dynamic Side of Philosophy: Here the great scholars like Ghazali, Iqbal, Plato, and Aristotle wanted that their philosophies should be given practical shape. The shape can be given only through well planned education system.

vi) Sound mind in Sound Body or Virtuous Man: The main purpose of education is to have sound mind in a sound body, and virtuous person. Philosophy gives answers and discuss that what is sound mind, sound body, and what virtuous person is. How we can say the philosophy is the contemplative aspect of education and education is the dynamic aspect philosophy.

vii) Change in Education, Culture and Society: In order to bring the desire change in society or in the existing education set up, a very pre-planned philosophy should be behind that kind of reformation. Like the western nations want reforms in our education system especially in madrasa through induction of computer and other subjects. This is pre-planned program in order to divert the students' attention from Quran, Hadith and Jehad lessons.

viii) Method of Functioning: Philosophers question the varied phenomena of the world in order to understand reality. However, education does not engage in such a procedure. Instead, it transmits knowledge and develops individual personalities.

The Interdependence of Philosophy and Education

Education is reliant of Philosophy because of following reasons:

(1) Philosophy Determines the Real Destination Towards Which Education needs to Go: Education is a cognizant dynamic process which need legitimate direction and supervision. Without legitimate direction and supervision, it cannot accomplish its objective. Philosophy determines the objectives of life and provides suitable and effective direction and supervision for education to accomplish that objective. Without the assistance of philosopher, education cannot be a fruitful interaction of development and accomplishment. Spencer has rightly remarked—"True education is practicable simply by a true philosophy".

(2) Philosophy Determines the Various Aspects of Education: Some researchers accept that philosophy is concerned with conceptual things and conceptions only, while education deals with practical, concrete things and processes. Subsequently, the two are extraordinary and there exists no relation between them. In any case, this is a wrong belief. Both philosophy and education are personally and essentially associated with one another. Separation between the two is beyond the realm of imagination regardless. It is the philosophy, we should know, that has been impacting all aspects of education since the very beginning and will continue affecting education for all times to come. Indeed, it will be better to recollect the saying of Ross that—"Philosophy and education are like the two sides of the same coin, present various perspectives on something very similar, and that one is implied by the other."

(3) Great Philosophers have been Great Educationists Also: History bears persuasive testimony to the fact that great philosophers have been extraordinary educationists likewise of their times. Plato, Socrates, Locke, Comenius, Rousseau, Froebel, Dewey, Gandhi, Tagore, Aurobindo Ghosh and other people who were great philosophers of their times have likewise discussed about education. Their philosophical compositions have been important guidebooks for educational planning and determination of educational aims for children of the world. As such, all great philosophers have employed education as a means to translate their philosophical thoughts into practice for the individuals to follow and develop themselves.

Philosophy is dependent on Education due to following reasons:

(1) Education is the Dynamic Side of Philosophy: Two things are essential for finishing any task (a) Thought or plan and (b) Application or practicability. Philosophy is the idea or plan side and education is the application or pragmatic side. Philosophy decides the aim of life and by analysis lays down the principles to be followed for accomplishing the set aims. Education deciphers these principles and ideas into practice because the purpose of education is to mould human behaviour. Consequently, Adams has rightly said - "Education is the dynamic side of philosophy."

(2) Education is a way to Achieve the Goal: As said above it is philosophy which decides the aims of life. Through analysis and classification these are divided into objectives to be accomplished by the process of education. Herbart holds the similar opinion – "Education has no time to make holiday till all the philosophical questions are once for all cleared up". At times educationists and educators put before philosophers such issues which face them and defy solutions. Thusly, education contributes to new way of thinking and new philosophy may born out of his thinking and analysing. So close are these two, the philosophy and the education, that it will be better and smarter to talk this relation in more prominent as Philosophy and Aims of Education, Philosophy and Curriculum, Philosophy and Methods of teaching. Philosophy and Disciplines. Philosophy and Textbooks, etc.

Why does Teacher need to Study the Philosophy of Education?

The role of a teacher apart from teaching academics is his/her active role as a mentor in inculcating independent thinking in student. But before we the teachers who start our journey as a mentor need to develop our own teaching philosophy. It is very obvious for the students to look up to their teachers and so it becomes very essential for the teachers to prepare themselves a role model to inspire the students. Now, as a teacher, if one needs to develop his/her own philosophy, then one needs to study the philosophy of education. And below is the answer to why a teacher should read the philosophy of education.

1.To encode the meaning of learning: Teaching the word can never be assessed in a single. Teaching the terms remains incomplete without learning. Thus one needs a direction to know how one can reach learning through teaching. That means one needs a map, which provides direction to move ahead. It is not possible to make students learn something until the teacher knows why and how he/she wants to teach. As soon as you know why and how to teach, you help your students to plan to reach their destinations.

2. Help society: As education is the backbone of society, the teachers are the builders of persons to prepare and strengthen the backbone. Teachers are considered the future makers of the community. They help students to select better professions. Every good teacher leaves a profound impact on their students and helps to build in them the power for taking independent decisions. The values that the student learn from their teachers today will be applied and used in society as they grow up. If being a teacher you are behaving rationally on the basis of a philosophy of your own, your students will definitely follow the path and they will behave rationally and will try to find out the answers to all whys. This attitude in students will develop the intellectual ability of the students.

3.Identify their qualities: Philosophy helps a teacher to analyse a students behaviour and actions. This helps the teacher to adopt better teaching methods, strategies and prepare timely guidance, eventually resulting in improved results. Added to this, a teacher would also be able to analyse his actions and understand the positives and negatives of their methods. The study of philosophy or the knowledge of philosophy helps not only the students but the teachers as well.

4. Helps to avoid being judgmental: Philosophy of education also helps teacher for considering the actions of each student. It helps the teacher to read the personality of each student. At the same time, the teacher should be conscious enough not to affect the unique potentialities and capabilities of each student. As a mentor and educator, you are required to teach creativity, autonomy and curiosity to all students without compromising their intellectual levels. Philosophy repeats that a teacher should culture an unbiased attitude.

5. Inculcate the concept of togetherness: The teacher is a pivotal factor for unifying the students with himself/herself. He/she must ensure harmony among the students. Keeping the moral values intact, the students must be taught to serve society diligently.

6.The verdict: Apart from giving academic knowledge, it is necessary for a teacher to enrich the personal values of the students for their better upbringing at the present time to ensure a better future.

Conclusion

From the discussions it became clear that philosophy and man are interdependent. From man's true nature as an essentially controversial, problematic and historical being, the nature of philosophy as an essentially critical, reflective and open discipline establishes itself. It also becomes clear that, because man is essentially controversial, problematic and historical, philosophy can in reality never vacate. Where the conscious attempt is made to abolish philosophy by reduction to the descriptive method or to one or other act of man, this leads to the suppression in some form or another of the reflective and differentiating individual, and thus to an unauthentic way of human existence. Since, however, the attempt at the rejection of philosophy in whatever form does not really lead to its disappearance, because any such attempt takes place by philosophical reflection and emerges as another theory which is philosophical in character, philosophy, as a reflective science, cannot be replaced by any such attempt. Such an attempt is mainly made with the aim of avoiding philosophical confusion and controversy.

CHAPTER THREE

PHILOSOPHY OF EDUCATION AND ITS IMPLICATIONS

Introduction

Education can be thought of as the transmission of the values and accumulated knowledge of the society. As society grows more complex, the quantity of knowledge to be passed on from one generation to the next generation too increases. Similarly as society gradually attaches more and more importance to education, it also tries to formulate the overall objectives, content, organization and strategies of education. In short, there is development in philosophy and theories of education.

According to Socrates-"Education means bringing out of the idea of universal validity which is latent in the mind of every man".

According to Knowels (1995), education is the development of all those capabilities in which the individual which is enable him to control his environment and fulfillment his possibilities.

According to Mrunalini (2010), education is the process of changing behavior pattern of people acquisition of the art of utilization of knowledge and ideas.

Thus, the education is the process of facilitating learning, or the acquisition of knowledge, skills, values,beliefs, and habits. Education is the development of all those capabilities in which the individual which is enable him to control his environment and fulfillment his possibilities.

Meaning of philosophy

Philosophy is an academic discipline that exercises reason and logic in an attempt to understand reality and answer fundamental questions about knowledge, life, morality and human nature. Philosophy is a comprehensive system of ideas and it is at the root of all knowledge. It is a continuous seeking of insight into basic realities the physical world, mind, society, knowledge and values.

The word "philosophy" comes from the Greek word "philosophia", which combines the words "philo" meaning "love of" and "sophia" meaning "wisdom". It is commonly held that the word philosophy was first used by the Greek philosopher Pythagoras circa 500 B.C. The term was often contrasted with the word "Sophistry" which literally translates to "wise man". The latter indicates one's concern knowledge, while the former indicates a love of truth. Philosophy is the rational investigation of logic, ethics, and metaphysics. Philosophy is essentially a spirit or method of approaching experience rather than a body of conclusions.

Philosophy is a study that seeks to understand the mysteries of existence and reality. It tries to discourse the nature of truth and knowledge and to find what is of basic value and importance in life. It also examines the relationship between humanity and nature and between individual and society. Philosophy arises out of wonder, curiosity, and the desires to know and understand.Thus philosophy is a form of inquiry-a process of analysis, criticism, interpretation and speculation

Philosophy of Education and Its Implications

Philosophy is the study of the principles of human behavior and reasoning about we really know of the human behavior and reasoning about we really know of the universe and ourselves. It means, philosophy is that through which man tries to understand him and the world in which he/she views. Major systems of philosophy of education are:

Idealism:it is oldest system of philosophy known to man. Its origin goes back to ancient India in the east, and to Plato in the west. Its basic viewpoint stresses the human spirit as the most important element in life. The human spirit is most elements in life, the universe is essentially non-material in its ultimate nature. Idealism is concerned with supremacy of mind and self, and views man and universe in terms of spirit or mind. Matter or objective may be the projection or creation of mind, but ultimately real is the idea behind it.

The physical world is ephemeral and can be changed through the ideas or imagination of man. Plato, the greatest philosopher of all ages, claimed that the ultimate reality consists of ideas. Plato and his teacher Socrates conceived ideas as the basis of their philosophy. Socrates, an idealistic philosopher placed importance on question-answer and dialogue as the method of acquiring information or gaining knowledge whereas Plato emphasized on logical reasoning as the method of gaining knowledge.

Educational Implications of Idealism

Idealism considers student as an individuals with inner potentials. Education should help the student to realize these potentials. Curriculum should consist of those knowledge and experiences which help the student to attained development. The teacher should impart essentials of knowledge and assist to develop moral and aesthetic values in the child. As said earlier, idealism stresses more on the spiritual development of the child.

Naturalism

It is oldest philosophy in western world. The naturalist's views the world that we live in is made up of the matters, and believes that the material world, the world of nature, is the real world. In other word nature is the source of knowledge. The human life is the part of nature and is therefore controlled by external laws of nature. In fact, the essence of all things is nature. The universe and man are the results of physical, mechanical and biological forces acting upon them, which are called natural laws. The process of growth and development in man was the result of force of energy prevailed in nature. Man's natural endowment, including his instincts and emotion are the guiding force of all his conducts.The theory of struggle put forward by Charles Darwin implicates that the aim of education is to equip individual to struggle for existence and thus to ensure his survival. It should help the learner to adjust physically and mentally to ever changing circumstances of life. Education should aim at developing the child joyful, rational, balanced, purposeful and mature person in order for him to survive.

Educational implications of naturalism

Applied to education, naturalism considers child as a gift of nature with potentialities for natural growth according to laws of nature. The child is an active individual capable of self- development. The aim of education is to develop the child as healthy and active personality in a natural setting. The growth process must be natural and real without any interference from outside. The powers of the child should be developed in natural ways by allowing the child to freely interact with the nature.

The curriculum should provide concrete and real experiences in a natural context. The child should be exposed to a variety of sensory and physical activities. The child learns by interacting with nature. Morality and character learned directly with the help of natural consequences. Discipline is developed as a result of consequences of behavior of child. The teacher plays the role of guiding the child learning from nature.

Realism

The term 'realism', derived from the world 'real', finds its origin in Greek word: 'Res '' which means object. The realistic propagates that we see and experience around us is the truth. The realistic propagates the world as nature rather than supernatural. The realistic believe that the physical universe is operated by natural laws. Aristotle (384-322 B.C.), a Greek philosopher is generally recognized as the father of realism.

The purpose of education was to prepare for complete living, the Realists believed. Education should equip the learners with the knowledge and skills that are needed to understand and master his physical environment so that he can live a happy and comfortable life.

Educational Implications of Realism

Realism considers the child as a dynamic and growing entity ready to face reality of life. The laws of nature control the child. The aim of education is to prepare the child to face. Hence the realists suggest that the curriculum should be broad based and include variety of subjects, especially science subjects. While selecting the subjects, the learner's background and social demand should be considered. Realism suggests objective methods of teaching. Importance must be given to observation, experimentation and activities. According to realism discipline is developed by controlling environment.

Pragmatism

Pragmatism adopts a midway between idealism and naturalism. The word pragmatism derived from Greek word "pragma" means action. Pragmatism is otherwise known as instrumentalism or functionalism. Since emphasis was given to learning by doing and learning by experience, it is also called experimentalism.

According to Ross, pragmatism is essentially a human philosophy maintaining that man creates his own values in course of activity, that reality is still in making and awaits its part of completion from the future. This definition emphasis on creation through continuous activity and states that certain values are essential for growth and development of individual.

Educational Implication of Pragmatism

Pragmatism trend in education is known as progressivism in education and the school based on programmatic ideas was known as progressive school. Pragmatism considers the learner as growing biological and social being ready to adjust to the environmental demands. The aim of education should be to prepare the child to become an effective member of community. It should also try to develop competencies in the child. Hence the curriculum should include those subjects and experience which are suitable to the child's interest and needs. The curriculum should be develop an attitude of inquiry, facilitate artistic expression, encourage constructiveness and sustain interest in the child. Deway advocates "learning by doing", which encourages the child to learn trough activities. Deway considers discipline as a function of the teaching- learning situation. If the learning is made joyful and interesting, there is no need to use external rewards and punishments. A pragmatic teacher helps in the ready-made forms; teacher should encourage the learner through active interaction with the learning situation.

Conclusion

All educational activities, from classroom practice to curriculum decisions to the setting of policies at the school, district, state, and central levels, inevitably rest upon philosophical assumptions, claims, and positions. Consequently, thoughtful and defensible educational practice depends upon philosophical awareness and understanding. To that extent, the philosophy of education is essential to the proper guidance of educational practice. Knowledge of philosophy of education would benefit not only teachers, administrators, and policy makers at all levels but also students, parents, and citizens generally. Societies that value education and desire that it be conducted in a thoughtful and informed way ignore the philosophy of education at their peril. Its relevance, reach, and potential impact make it perhaps the most fundamental and wide-ranging area of applied philosophy. Thus the philosophy, importance and implications of education process in our contemporary environment as well as the world and people acquire knowledge, ideas, and skills and utilize to those knowledge and ideas for the development and prosperity of humankind as well as the development of nation and the entire world.

CHAPTER FOUR

EDUCATION IN VEDIC AND POST VEDIC PERIOD

Introduction

The education system which was evolved first in ancient India is known as the Vedic system of education . In other words, the ancient system of education were based on the Vedas and therefore it was given the name of Vedic Educational system. Some scholars have sub divided Vedic Educational period into Rig- Veda period, Brahmani period,Upanishada period, Sutra (Hymn) period, Smriti period etc but all these period, due to predominance of the Vedas, there was no change in the aims and ideals of educations. That is why, the education of these periods, is studied under Vedic period.

" Swadesh Pujyate Raja, Vidwan SarvatraPujyate"

The Education system of Vedic period has unique characteristics and qualities which were not found in the ancient education system of any other country of the world. According to Dr. F. E.key, "To achieve their aim not only did Brahmans develop a system of education which, survived even in the events of the crumbling of empires and the changes of society, but they, also through all those thousands of years, kept a glow of torch of higher learning".

Purpose of studying Vedas

Vedas occupy a very important place in the Indian life. The basis of Indian culture lies in the Vedas which are four in number - Rigveda, samveda, Yajurveda, and Atharavaveda.

(1) Rigveda:"RIK" means Parise. Rigveda contains praises for the dieties like indra, agni, Rudra and the two Ashwini gods, Varuna, Maruti,Savitru and Surya. Tapping the energies of the nature is given high importance in Rigveda. It contains 1017 hymns (poems) to it praise the gods.

(2) Yajurveda:'Yajuish'means rituals. Yajurveda contains different rituals and sacrifices to be conducted to pacify gods. When a mantra is recited and it's power is felt, then to make the mantra useful, a certain type of offerings to be done to the concerned god. Yajurveda explains about these offerings to be made to gods through Agni (fire).

(3) Sama veda :'sama' means song. Samveda contains verses to be sung. These verses are built in their root from using the 7 notes. Sa, Re, Ga, Ma, Pa, Dha, Ni which are the basis of the classical music now existing in India. These notes aid the liberation of soul by stimulating the energycentres (chakras) in the human body.

(4) Atharavaveda: Atharavaveda contains useful rituals to attain worldly happiness. It contains description of diseases, how to cure them, sins and how to remove their effects and means of acquiring wealth. Atharavaveda is more applicable to modern society since it deals with different subjects like science, Medicine, Mathematics, Engineering, Technology etc.

The knowledge and wisdom of the Vedas is said to have been revealed by God to the enlightened ones. The Vedas have been translated in almost all the major languages of the world. The meaning of Veda in his book Krishna Yajurveda. According to Sayan Veda is a symbol of that thing through which one attains his objective and protects oneself from bad traits, undesirable things and behaviours.

Vedas have their own characteristics features. Through them we are able to know about the culture, civilization life and philosophy of people in ancient India. Vedas symbolise the chief objective of human life which has been deliberance from this world of truths and deaths. This objective has always been unchangeable. The Indian philosophy of life, has never accepted life as purposeless. The deliberance of soul has been the chief objective of this philosophy of life from time Immemorial. This fact is very clear from the study of Rigveda.

The Vedas are intended to serve a different purpose they have to be learnt by heart understanding the correct way of pronouncing the Mantra, by listening to the rendering of the Mantras by the guru (teacher). The Vedas mantra so learnt should become the guide in our Karma-aanushtaana, Tapas, Isvara aaradhana etc.If, in India, the Vedas retain their original vitality even today, it is because these hymns are being continuously repeated by Student and teachers of the Vedas, and the purity of the sounds and accents of the world's are retained in that process.

Acceptable feature of Education of Vedicperiod for modernEducation

There is wide gap of Education between Ancient Indian Education and modern Indian Education. Still there are several elements of ancient education which can find room in modern education both in theory and practice.

Idealism: We are living in modern age but we feel pound of the civilization and culture of our ancestors inherited to us. Even now we give importance to religion,good and desireless deeds. We give more preference to character,spiritualism, philosophy rather than wealth, materialism and science.

Discipline and Teacher-Pupil Relationship: The sense of discipline and the cordial relation between teacher and Pupil of Vedic age is well know to the world today we see the educational environment has become so venomous due to indiscipline that is has become an uncountable problem.

Subject of studies: The study of Sanskrit language and Sanskrit literature in neglected to a grater extent. It is this literature which is enriched by the sense of peace, humanity, universal brotherhood which should be vital part of our curriculum.

Teaching Method: In ancient period Shravan or Listening. Manan or meditation and Nididhyaana or realization and experience, question and answers, discourse, lecture discussion and debate methods were prevalent. These methods can be still used in our classrooms faithfully.

Free and Universalization of Education: Education was free and universal. The free, if any, was to be paid, after attaining education from the earnings of the young man who got education, in the from of 'Guru Dakshina'. During education the boarding and lodging was free for almost all these students. After independence our constitution framers made it clear that it is the duty of all government to provide free education to every child of 0-14 yes age group. Many programme for this cause has been adopted but still desired objective has not been achieved.

Thus we can say that the education of Vedic age has it's significance in Modern age.

Characteristics of Educational System

In Vedic era education had a very prominent place in society. It was being considered as pious and important for society. In the eyes of Aryans, education was the only means to acquire, prosperity in the field of physical,mental, spiritual and social developments. Education was must for everybody for becoming cultured. Education was an instrument to show new paths and knowledge to us . Education opens our hidden qualities and helps people to attain Salvation.It can be regarded as "Third Eye" of human beings. Through education only a man gets rid from debt of Guru and so was the feeling of people at that time.

The main Characteristics of Vedic education can be briefly enumerated as follows:

Knowledge: Education is knowledge.It is man's third eye . This aphorism means that knowledge opens man's inner eye, flooding him with spiritual and divine light, which forms the provision for man's journey through life. Through education , the development of every aspect of human life become possible. Knowledge projects an individual like a mother, inspires him to follow the path of good conduct as father does, and gives the pleasure that one's wife provides.

Aims of Education: The ultimate aim of education in ancient Indian was not knowledge as preparation for life in this world or for life beyond, but for complete realization of self for liberation of the soul from the chains of life both present and future. During this period, education had an idealistic from, in which the teachers (acharyas) laid stress upon worship of God, religiousness, spirituality, formation of character, development of personality, creation of an aptitude for the development of culture, nation and society.

Methods of Instruction: It was a Pupil centered education. No single method of instruction was adopted, though recitation by the Pupil followed by explanation by the teacher, was generally followed. Besides question – Answer, Debate and Discussion, Story telling was also adopted according to need.There was no classroom teaching.However monitorial system was prevalent and senior pupils were appointment to teach Junior's. Travel was regarded as necessary to give finishing touch to education so the methods of teaching generally practiced during Vedic period we're mainly Maukhik and other method was based on Chintan.

Practicability: Apart from intellectual aspect of education it's practical side was not lost sight of and along with art, literature and philosophy, Students got a working knowledge of animal husbandry, agriculture and other professions of life. In addition education in medicine was also imported.

Education for the Individual: The nature of education was much more individualistic rather than joint in groups. All round development of a child's Personality was the chief aim of education. Every teacher devoted himself to be integral development of each student.

Duration of Education: In the house of the teacher, the student was required to obtain education up to the age of 24, after which he was expected to enter domestic life. Student were divided into three categories:These obtaining education up to the age of 24- Vasu; These obtaining education up to the age of 36- Rudra and These obtaining education up to the age of 48- Auditya.

Curriculum: Although the education of this period was dominated by the study of Vedic Literature, historical Study, stories of heroic lives and discourses on the puranas also formed a part of the syllabus. Students had necessarily to obtain knowledge of metrics. Arithmetic was supplemented by the knowledge of geometry. Students were given knowledge of four Vedas – Rigveda, Yajurveda, Samaveda and Atharavaveda. The syllabus took with in its compass such subjects as spiritual as well as materialistic knowledge, Vedas, Vedic grammar, arthimetic knowledge of gods, knowledge of the absolute, knowledge of ghosts, astronomy, logic philosophy ethics, conduct etc. The richness of the syllabus was responsible of the creation of Brahman literature in this period.

Commercial Education and Mathematics Education: Commercial education and mathematics education is also one of the chief features of Vedic period. The ideas of the scope and nature of commercial education can be held from Manu. Knowledge of Commercial geography, needs of the people of various localities, exchange value and quality of articles and language spoken at different trade center were considered necessary. Theory of banking was also included in the course. Though there were no organized educational institutional training was usually imparted in the family.

As far as Mathematics education is concerned, ancient Indian quite early evolved simple system of geometry. Shulva sutra are the oldest mathematical works probably compassed between 400 BC and 200 A.D. Aryabhata (476.52 BC) is the first great name in Indian Mathematics. The concept of Zero also belong to this period.

Education in Post Vedic Period

To attain Salvation by realizing the truth has been the aims to education during this period only that education was regarded true which helped one be realize this supreme truth. According to the Upanishads 'truth', alone is the knowledge and the other worldly knowledge is untruth. The worldly knowledge was regarded as ignorance. Upanishads maintain that one cannot attain Salvation through worldly knowledge because through this, one becomes involved in illusion (Maya).

Chief Features of post –Vedic Education:

1) UpanayanSanskar: Upanayan Sanskar was considered important both in the Vedic and post Vedic periods.This is evident at several place in the Rigveda. But different values were adhered to in two periods. It was not necessary during the Vedic period to have the upanayan ceremony before starting education.

2) The Important Place of the Teacher: During this period the teacher (Guru) enjoyed a predominant place not only in his Gurukul but in the entire society. To his pupils he showered all love and affection and use to teach them whatever he knew, but before doing this he always tested the deservingness of a particular Pupil.

3) Curriculum during post-Vedic Period: During this period the curriculum included more subject than during the Vedic age. Ved Mantras (hymns and verses) we're principally taught in the Vedic period. During the post- Vedic period various types of Literature's were produced pertaining to the different Vedas . In addition to religious subjects, many worldly subjects were also included in the curriculum. It consisted of Vedas, History, Puranas, Grammar, Mathematics, Braham-Vidya, Nirukti, astronomy, dance, music etc. Question answer system prevailed during his period. Through this system difficult and abstract ideas were made simple.

Duration of Education: Duration of education during the post Vedic period was almost the same as in the Vedic age. The duration was of about twelve years although the number of subjects of Study we're increased.

Women's Education: Many changes were introduced in women education during post-Vedic period. This led to fall of women education . During the Vedic age the women enjoyed equal educational right. During post Vedic period they were deprived of the social and religious functions.

Varnasystem and Education in society: The Varna system in the Vedic age was based on one's work or duty (Karma). During Vedic period one could choose a particular profession as he liked and accordingly his Varna came to be determined. But during the post Vedic period Varna came to be determined by birth. Consequently the whole society was divided in to four varnas–Brahman, Kshatriyas, Vaishyas, & Shudra.

Educational Achievements of Vedic age were as follows:

1. Education emphasized the development of spirituality the ashram system was adopted for paying of the individual debt towards the Goods, his forefathers, his teacher and society.

2. The minds of parents were first prepared to instill in them a desire for the education of their children. It has been said that those parents are the enemy of the child who do not teach their children.

3. Education was free. It's expenses were born by the society and the king.

4. White living an Gurukul the child imbibed education in a favourable environment.

5. A student was compelled to obey the ideals of the Gurukul. He had to shoulder the burden of existence through begging for alms. This practice developed humility and tolerate in the student.

6. During the period vocational education was also in Vogue Military, Science, Agriculture, Animal Husbandry, Veterinary Science, Medicine etc were among the subjects taught. Chemistry was also taught. Arts and Handicrafts were highly respected. Education in Commerce was very popular.

Conclusion

Lastly we may conclude that the Vedic education being mostly spiritual, liberal and contemplative in nature, was meant for all who were really interested, capable and dedicated and we're in search of the highest truth and supreme knowledge. Education was free of cost and the students led an exemplary life in Vedic system of education. The teacher - taught relationship was very cordial and just like the father – son relationship during Vedic period. Education was not based on cast, Creed, colour and religion.

CHAPTER FIVE

IMPACT OF IDEALISM ON EDUCATION

Introduction

The term Idealism is the combination of the words- 'Idea' and 'Ism'. It is the synonym of the English word 'Idealism'. Idealism may be derived from 'ideas' or 'ideals. In other words, idealism is originated from Plato's Theory of Ideas. According to this doctrine only ideas are of supreme importance. The real word is 'ideaism' but the letter "l" added to aid in the pronunciation and hence it is known as Idealism.

Idealism holds that material world is destructible and mortal. Behind the material world there is another world which is indestructible and immortal. This is known as spiritual world. They deny the supreme importance of matter. According to them only spiritual values are immortal and true. Man's spiritual nature considered to be the very essence of his being. Idealism holds that material and physical universe is incomplete without the mental world. Nothing is more real and true apart from human mind.

The supporters of Idealism are Plato, Socrates, Descartes, Comenius, Berkley, Kant, Froebel, Mahatma Gandhi, Rabindranath Tagore, Swami Vivekananda, Aurobindo Ghosh and S. Radhakrishnan. They have expressed their views and made their contribution on Idealistic field of education.

Idealism denies the supreme importance of man. Spiritualism is the ultimate reality according to Idealism. It is true that mind is beyond everything. Human mind is more valuable than his physical appearance. Even a blind man can perceive the world through his mind. It is soul which speaks not body. From this point of view the philosophy of Idealism has much relevance in the present era. Idealism lays stress on self-realization. It is self which is to be educated first. A child must have deeper understanding of his self through which he can know himself thoroughly. Self-realization leads to exaltation of human personality. It is true that today our country needs great personalities to form a better society. Thus, from this angle study of Idealism is essential. Idealist's emphasis on moral and spiritual values helps in solving present day educational problems. Today our society is facing a lot of crisis. At this juncture future citizens should be given value education and darkness of materialism should be removed. It is said that character of the child is to be formed first. The curriculum of idealism includes study of ethics, religion, morality, culture which helps in the development of character of the child. Like Idealism today's schools do not follow any specific method of teaching. Many institutions have adopted the idea of self-discipline for spiritual conduct of the child. Not only child but an ideal teacher can walk on the path of idealism in order to provide fruitful education to students. So, from all these perspectives study of idealism is the need of the hour.

Main features of Idealism: The main features of Idealism are: -

ax. Spirit and mind only constitute reality.

ax. Material or Physical universe is not real and is perishable.

ax. God is the source of all knowledge and creations found in the world.

ax. Human body is false as it is mortal: soul is true as it is immortal.

ax. Nothing exists except what exists in the Absolute Mind of which finite minds are parts.

ax. Truth, beauty and goodness are the eternal values which are essential qualities of human being.

ax. Apart from general education it gives more importance to moral and spiritual education.

ax. The source of attaining true knowledge is wisdom or intellectual enlightenment.

ax. The ultimate reality lies in not the object itself but the idea or ideal behind it.

ax. As man has the highest power of intelligence within him through which he can modify his environmental surroundings, Idealists attach more importance to man, the supreme work of God.

Forms of Idealism- The different forms of Idealism are: -

1. Subjective Idealism- Berkeley is the chief exponent of this view. According to him only mind is real. Even attributes and qualities are mental in nature. The physical world is only an appearance and that things exists and have their reality only when they are being perceived by infinite minds of which finite minds are parts. Apart from perceiving mind they have no reality and existence.

2. Absolute Idealism- Fitche and Hegel are the exponents of absolute Idealism. According to them only self (soul) is the absolute reality. All events in the universe are governed by some absolute laws. Therefore, only absolute laws are real. Hegel's absolute idealism regards universe as a great thought process.

3. Objective Idealism- Plato is the originator of this objective idealism. He argues that spirit is independent of realization. Whether anyone considers or not God is real and will always remain real. All souls have their independent existence. Objective Idealism holds, God and souls are inseparable. "There is no God without world and there is no world without God".

4. Phenomenal Idealism- Kant is the advocate of Phenomenal Idealism. He opined that knowledge acquired through physical or meta physical world is not absolutely real. It is only the phenomenon of the reality. Original or absolute reality cannot be discovered by human beings as it is beyond their capacities. Even the knowledge of God, heaven or hell cannot be known by anybody.

Idealism and Education- Idealism holds that true reality lies in spiritual being and not on material things. Only universal ideas and eternal values have independent existence. Therefore, the task of education should be to realize those absolute ideas and values.

Man is the creator of his own spiritual environment. He never satisfied with what he has. He wants more and more intellectually and culturally. Day by day his thirst for intellectual knowledge is increasing. Spiritual or cultural knowledge is to be acquired by man himself. Here lies the importance of education whose main aim is to transmit from one generation to another the spiritual or cultural heritage of man. Education must foster this development of cultural inheritance. Education must enable man to harmonize with truth, beauty and goodness.

Idealism and aims of education- Idealists have summarizes the aims of education in the following way. These are: -

Self-realization- Self-realization is one of the most important aim of education according to Idealism. As Idealists attach great importance to spiritual self it lay great stress on the exaltation of human personality or self-realization. Self-realization involves full knowledge of the self. For example, Shankaracharya says, "Education is the realization of the self". Aurobindo Ghosh remarks, "Education helps the growing soul to draw out that is in itself". Hence according to Idealism, the chief aim of education is to exalt human personality which implies realization of highest abilities and potentialities in a socio-cultural environment. Thus, a fruitful environment should be provided to the educand which will enable him to realize his inner self.

Universal education- As education is the birth right of every human being so according to Idealism education should be universal in nature. For establishment of a better society every man should be given the opportunity to discover his inner potentialities. In order to achieve this aim of education Idealists are in favour of universalization of education. It is only universalization of education which leads man towards betterment of society.

Spiritual development- Spiritual development is one of the most important aim of education according to Idealism. The school environment should be prepared in such a way so that each child develops mentally, morally and above all spiritually.

Physical development- The health and fitness of the body much receive special attention without which spiritual development is impossible. A sound mind rest in a sound body. Along with general education physical aspects of education should be taken into consideration which will help in the development of personality.

Intellectual development- The child should not be developed physically only but also intellectually. Education will create such an environment for the child which will help him to nurture his qualities both physically and intellectually. It may enable the child to achieve the highest aim by developing his creative potentialities and adjust with his environment.

Moral development- Idealists have attached great importance to the morality of the child. It is only through moral development spiritual development of the child is possible. Through such development child will able to distinguish between right and wrong. The child will proceed towards right path and avoids the wrong one. Thus, a child who is morally educated can lead towards progress of society.

Preservation and transmission of culture- A man's development is incomplete without his cultural upliftment. It is education which transmits cultural values from one generation to another. Thus, the aim of education according to idealism, is to acquaint the child with cultural heritage so that he can conserve, promote and transmit to the next generation.

Development of inventive and creative powers- It is only man who can change and modify his environment according to his needs and requirements. Therefore, the task of education should be to develop the inner creative powers in man which should be inventive in nature and will enable man to make his adjustment with the surrounding environment.

Simple living and high thinking- Simple living and high thinking is one of the important idealistic aim of education. In order to lead a better life mind should be developed, controlled and trained. A balanced mind is essential to lead a life of simple living and high thinking.

Cultivation of truth, beauty and goodness- A child should be encouraged to cultivate truth, beauty and goodness to achieve self-realization. These three values determine three types of human activities- intellectual, aesthetic and moral.

Idealism and Curriculum- The realization of aims of education will remain incomplete without a well-developed curriculum. Idealists gave first preference to thoughts, feelings, ideals and values of a child than his physical activities while designing a curriculum. The three highest values such as truth, goodness and beauty should be included as a part of the curriculum which determines four types of human activities- intellectual, moral, aesthetic and physical. Thus, subjects like humanities, languages, physical sciences, social sciences, metaphysics, ethics, religion and aesthetic activities like art and poetry should be included as an integral part of the curriculum.

Idealists also attach great importance to physical education. For this, it takes into account the study of hygiene and physiology and the practice of physical skills such as gymnastics and aesthetics. Besides this, art, music, dance, drawing and teaching of science which will develop the willing faculty and doing capacity of mind should be included in the curriculum. For promoting moral and spiritual values subjects like literature, history, poetry, political economy, study of religion, culture, sociology, handicrafts etc. should be given utmost importance which will not only promote social development but will lead cultural enrichment.

Idealism and method of teaching- Idealists does not have any specific method of teaching. Based upon child's interest they follow different methods of teaching. These are: -

Question-answer method- Socrates used question-answer method. Through this method the child will answers to various questions and thus enriched his knowledge and experience.

Discussion method- Plato emphasized discussion method which will help in the development of will power and concentration of the child.

Inductive-deductive method- Aristotle advocated Inductive-deductive method through which child will develop logical reasoning and analysis.

Simple to Complex method- Descartes employed the device of simple to complex method. In this method materials should be presented in such away so that a child will proceed from simple to complex and vice-versa.

Observation method- Pestalozzi emphasized on observation method. Through observation the child's sense organ will be stimulated. He said, "I want to psychologize education and Instruction".

Play-way method- Froebel advocated play-way method. He devised various gifts and occupations through which faculties of mind are strengthened and improved to a great extent.

Instruction method- Herbert advocated Instruction method. Instruction method helps the child to learn and imitate many things in his natural surroundings.

Other methods included narration, explanation, exposition, practice and repetition through which child acquires self-education.

Idealism and the teacher- The teacher occupies a very prestigious role in Idealistic Philosophy of education. He enjoys a respectable position in the whole process of education. His place is next to God. He is a friend, philosopher and the guide. He teaches the child how to proceed from darkness of ignorance and superstition to light. Teacher is like guru. The relation between the teacher and taught is that of like father and son. The immature learner cannot attain perfection of his personality unless there is someone to lead him to perfection. It is the teacher who play the role of advisor, director and controlling the conduct of his pupil so that he may ensure the perfection of his personality. The teacher should possess a high standard of behavior and a deep knowledge of his subject. According to Gentile "Teacher is a spiritual symbol of right conduct". Just like the parents Teacher's love, affection and sympathy is equally important for the growing child. Froebel states, "The school is a garden, the teacher is a cautious gardener and the child is a tender plant. The plant can grow no doubt without help but a good gardener sees that the plant grows to the finest possible perfection".

Idealism and the child- Idealism prepares the child for a holy life. In idealistic education the inculcation of highest values such as truth, goodness and beauty are more important than any other values. This will lead to the development of moral character of the child. The idealist considers student to remain under the supervision of teacher. The student should obey their teacher. They should have the feeling of love, respect and dedication towards their teacher. The relation between the teacher and taught should be cordial in nature.

Idealism and discipline- Idealism reject the concept of free discipline. According to them without strict discipline spiritual development is impossible. Excessive freedom can ruin the personality of the child. The habit of self-discipline should be developed among the child. Children should be encouraged to participate in creative activities. Self-discipline enables the child to develop self-confidence. It is only through self-discipline student's personality can be well developed. Humility, respectfulness and subservience are the other qualities through which child can be grown up into a better adult. Thomas and Lang have rightly stated, "Freedom is the cry of Naturalists while discipline is that of Idealists". Thus, Idealists crave for discipline.

Idealism and the school- According to Idealism school is a miniature society. The school of the idealists based on the principles of simple living and high thinking. It is a place where child's abilities, capacities and potentialities are progressively developed by teachers. The student should come to school not only for collecting information but to experience those things which will help in the development of his overall personality. School is a meeting place of the two souls- teacher and students. Idealism holds that the qualities of patriotism, humanity, devotion to God, religiousness in the minds of the students can be developed through prayers and teaching personalities of great men. It is in school only where spiritual learning can take place through self-education and self-realization.

Contributions of Idealism to education- The philosophy of Idealism has brought a revolutionary change in the field of education. It has contributed a lot towards educational theory and practice. It's influence upon the field of education can be judged through the following: -

Aim- Idealism has contributed much towards the aims of education. The aim of education is personality development through self-realization and creation of an ideal society. Modern curriculum and teaching methods has been shaped through these educational aims. As spiritual development is the ultimate aim of life modern school provides spiritual knowledge by imparting lessons on religious and moral education.

Curriculum- Modern school teaches curriculum based on idealistic principles. Nowadays subjects like literature, history, music, art, physical education and culture are taught in every school which reflect the highest creations of human mind and involve noblest expression of human ingenuity and creative intelligence.

Method of teaching- Method of teaching has been influenced to a great extent by idealistic principles. Today lecture, discussion, observation and instruction method has been adopted by most schools. Froebel's play-way method has been practiced in most of the nursery schools. Play education is the basis of modern teaching-learning techniques.

Teacher- The place of teacher cannot be overlooked. Idealism has stressed the ideal character of the teacher which is very important in bringing desirable changes in the behavior of the learner. According to Idealism an ideal teacher must possesses pride and respect towards his profession. He must guide his students with love, affection and sympathy. Today's students need modification of behavior which is only possible by imitating an ideal teacher.

Child- Idealism has recognized the individuality of the child which has been practiced in modern schools. Modern school lays stress on value-based education through which individuality of the child can be best developed. Today's school teaches every child to speak truth, beauty should be in mind, not in face and he or she must be good to all creatures in the world. Therefore, eternal values like truth, goodness and beauty are cultivated in the minds of every child.

Teacher-student relation- The intimate relationship between the teacher and taught has been followed by Idealistic Schools of philosophy. In order to develop a cordial relationship between the two, the ratio of teacher-student is being reduced today.

Discipline- The idea of self-discipline as advocated by Idealism has been adopted by most of the schools today. Indian philosophers like Mahatma Gandhi and Vivekananda also emphasized on the concept of self-discipline. In order to develop personality of the student's Indian schools today teaches self-discipline which helps in self-realization.

Universalization of education- Idealists supported universalization of education which today has been accepted by all philosophers, educationists and political leaders. Nowadays school provides education to every individual to face all challenges of life boldly and confidentially.

Historical importance- Idealistic philosophy has historical importance in the sense that it has been supported by many philosophers and educationists of both East and the West. Many educational schemes, plans and policies have their origin in Idealistic philosophy.

Demerits of Idealism:

ax. Idealists point out that mind is central in understanding the world. But this view is not absolutely correct and above criticism.

ax. Modern education ignores the idealistic aims of education which are abstract, impracticable and difficult to achieve.

ax. Concepts like ideals, mind and spirit have little relevance nowadays in classroom teaching.

ax. Idealism neglects the material world and put too much emphasis on spiritual world.

ax. As it put too much stress on spiritualism it neglects the psychological nature of the child. It does not take into account individual differences and special abilities of the pupil.

ax. Idealists regard the eternal values such as truth, beauty and goodness as permanent and unchangeable. But in reality, they are not absolute and change with time and environment.

ax. Idealism overemphasized humanities and ignores science and technology which is the basis of modern education.

ax. Idealism overlooked freedom and kept child under strict discipline. It places too much emphasis on teachers and gives child a secondary importance.

ax. Idealism fail to provide a child-centered curriculum and significant method of teaching.

ax. Idealism overlooked physical, industrial, social and electronic environment which are essential for achieving social progress.

ax. The philosophy of Idealism fails to work in the modern scientific world.

Merits of Idealism- Idealism has certain advantages. These are:

ax. Idealism provides a comprehensive view about educational aims, curriculum, method of teaching etc.

ax. Idealism promotes universal education to form a better society.

ax. The knowledge of self-realization helps in spiritual development of the child.

ax. Idealism emphasizes on moral and spiritual values like truth, goodness and beauty which are essential for peace of mind. In fact, human values, welfare, peace, happiness and satisfaction cannot be achieved without moral or spiritual values.

ax. Idealism assigned teacher a very important role in the educational process.

ax. It emphasizes on moral character and personality development of the child.

ax. Idealism leads human beings towards the path of simple living and high thinking.

The philosophy of Idealism has been supported by many educationists and philosophers of the world. Rusk is of the opinion that idealism is the most adequate of all the philosophies of education as it provides the noblest and highest aims for educational achievements.

Conclusion

Idealism made valuable contributions towards the field of education. It provides clear and direct guidelines in determining the aims of education, curriculum, method of teaching etc. The study of literature, art, morality, religion, music and cultivation of truth, goodness and beauty leads the child towards the path of creativeness. Its principles are effective in bringing about changes in the policy of education. Idealism never considers man as a great machine. Man has higher levels of intellectual powers through which he can change and modify his environment. Importance of universalization of education shows that Idealism is against caste-based education. In the world of stress and strain it is only idealistic philosophy that can create a spiritual environment for human peace and happiness. The concept of unity in diversity, universal brotherhood has become very relevant in these days to foster national integration and international understanding. It has solved various problems of educationists and philosophers in their respective fields. Thus, the philosophy of idealism plays a leading role in making education more purposeful and goal-oriented.

CHAPTER SIX

SAMKHYA PHILOSOPHY

Introduction

The Sāṁkhya Philosophy is one among the oldest school in India Philosophy. This is so because the basic tenets of Sāṁkhya can be seen in Nyāya, Vaiśeṣika, Yoga, Jainism, and Vedānta. The founder of Sāṁkhya Philosophy is 'Kapila' who has written the script 'Sāṁkhya Sūtra'. This script is widely known as Sāṁkhya Philosophy. It is commented by many scholars, out of those the significant commentary is known as 'Sāṁkhya Kārika' by Iśvarakṛsna. There are two views on the origin of this school. Some are believed that the word Sāṁkhya is derived from the word 'Saṁkhyā' which means number as well as right knowledge. Right knowledge is about understanding the reality by specifying the number of ultimate constituents of the universe. Others viewed that Sāṁkhya means 'perfect knowledge' and that is about the reality. With these introductions now let us know Sāṁkhya's metaphysics.

Metaphysics

The Sāṁkhya Philosophy is regarded as dualistic realism. It is dualistic because it holds the doctrine of two ultimate realities; Prakṛti and Purusas. Further, it maintains the plurality of Purusas (self) and the existence of matter, hence, treated as pluralistic. It is realism because they viewed that both matter and spirit are equally real. The Sāṁkhya school expresses that the self (Purusa) and the non-self (Prakriti) are radically different form each other, as like, subject and object. As subject can never be the object, similarly, an object can never be the subject. In this regard, a few important questions are addressed here. Those are, 'what is the ultimate cause of an object?' and, 'what are the constituents of the universe?' In other words, what is the ultimate stuff of which the various objects of the world are made? The Sāṁkhya replies that Prakriti is the ultimate (first) cause of all objects, including our mind, body and sense organs. It is observed that every effect must have a cause. Cause and effect are two inseparable components stand for all sorts of creation in the cosmos. Hence, all objects of the world are bounded in the chain of cause-effect relation. This relation Sāṁkhya named as 'satkāryavāda' and populated as 'theory of causation'.

Theory of Causation

The Sāṁkhya theory of causation is known as satk āryavāda. It explains the effect exists in its material cause prior to its production. For example, curd was existing in the milk before comes into existence. Hence, the effect is not a real beginning or a new creation. It is also named as 'parināmav āda'. By refuting this view Nyāyikas said that effect is a new creation, otherwise why we say this is the effect and that was the cause. The following arguments uphold by Sāmkhya to support the theory satkāryavāda.

- If the effect does not exist in the cause prior to its operation, none can bring into existence out of the cause. For example, blue cannot be turned into yellow even by a thousand artists. The effect is related to its cause. Effect is nothing but the manifestation of the cause, as oil will be produced from oil seeds only. Thus, effect pre-exists in the material cause in a latent or un-manifest condition.
- A particular effect can be produced out of a particular material cause. A mud jar can be produced out of clay only; cloth can be produced out of threads only. Thus, it proves that the effects are existing in the cause in a latent condition.
- If the effect is not related to its cause, then every effect would arise from every cause. But this does not happen. Every effect does not arise from every cause. For example, butter cannot be produced from sands, waters, or oils. It is produced from milk only.
- The effect pre-exists in the cause since it can be produced by a potent cause only. A potent cause has causal energy to produce a particular effect. The causal energy in this case is inferred from the perception of the effect. If the effect is not existent in the cause, then the causal energy can't be related to it. If the causal energy is unrelated to the effect, then any effect will arise from any cause. Hence, the effect must be pre-existent in its potent cause only.
- The effect pre-exists in the cause since it is identical in nature with its cause. The effect is not different from the cause. The cause is existent

and therefore, the effect cannot be non-existent. Hence, effect inheres in its cause. This is so because there is no identity between entity and non-entity.

The Sāṁkhya disagrees with Nyāyikas and said that if curd as an effect is a new creation and does not exist in its material cause (milk) prior to its production, then can we produce curd from some other liquids like oil, kerosene, diesel etc. Hence, each effect exists in its material cause prior to its production in a hidden form. Here, a question may come to your mind, i.e. if every effect must have a cause then what would be the cause of a material cause? By responding to this query Sāṁkhya philosophy expressed that Prakriti is the first and ultimate cause of all objects of the world both gross and subtle.

Prakṛti. Prakṛti is the ultimate cause of the universe. It is regarded as the first cause. All effects of the universe are based upon it. Being the first element of the universe, Prakṛti itself is uncaused, eternal, and all pervading. Hence, it is called "pradhāna". It can't be perceived but can be inferred from its effect. Thus, it is known as 'anumā'. In the form of conscious elements, it is called jada, and in the form of the unmanifested objects, it is called 'avayakta'.

Differences between Prakṛti and Objects. Objects are the effects of Prakṛti . These are dependant, relative, many and non-eternal because they are created and destroyed. But Prakṛti , on the other hand, has neither beginning nor end. It is unborn, independent, absolute, one, eternal and beyond creation and destruction. Objects are limited within the space-time continuum but Prakṛti is beyond of it. Objects are manifest and composite but Prakṛti is unmanifest and without parts. Thus, Vyāsa says that Prakṛti is both 'is' and 'is-not'.

Proofs for the existence of Prakṛti. There are five arguments offered by Isvarakrishna for the existence of Prakṛti. These are as follows;

ax. Every cause has its effect. Thus, cause and effect are distinct from each other although the effect exists in its material cause prior to its production (satkāryavāda). By implication therefore, the universe must have a cause. This cause unman fests the universe in its totality. This cause in nothing but the Prakṛti.

ax. Sāṁkhya satkāryavāda accepts the cause-effect relation as an inherence form which implies every effect inheres in its material cause. This holds that if the effect rolls back toward its cause, then it will dissolve in its cause. This helps to maintain the homogeneity in the universe. The balance universe from where everything manifold is regarded as Prakṛti.

ax. The activity is generated in the potent cause. All effects arise out of causes in which they were present in an unman fest form. Evolution means the manifestation of that which is involved. The world of objects which are effect must therefore be implicitly contained in some world cause.

ax. The world is an amalgam of all varieties of objects. However, some common qualities are found among all the objects. As a result, pleasure, pain, and indifference subsist among all varieties of objects. This implies that there should be a common cause which possesses these three qualities (pleasure, pain and indifference) and share in all the objects once they created. This cause is Prakṛti.

ax. The world is constituted of manifold of objects. The existence of all the objects must have a cause. This is so because they themselves can't be the cause of their creation. Further, they are limited, dependent, and relative and have an end. Hence, the cause which creates them should be unlimited, exists beyond creation and destruction, independent and eternal. Such a cause is the Prakṛti.

Gunas of Prakṛti. The Sāṁkhya Philosophy advocates three gunas of Prakṛti . These are; Sattva, rajas and tamas. Prakrti is a state of equilibrium of these three gunas. The word 'guna' is understood here as quality or attribute. Now, let us know about these three gunas.

ax. *Sattva.* Sattva is that element of Prakṛti which is of the nature of pleasure, light (laghu)and bright or illuminating (prakāsaka). The tendency towards conscious manifestation in the senses, the mind and the intellect; the luminosity of light and the power of reflection in a mirror or crystal are all due to the operation of the element of Sattva in the constitution of things. For example, blazing up a fire, upward curse of vapour etc. Sattva is believed to be white.

ax. *Rajas.* Rajas are the principle of activity in things. Its colour is red. It is active because ofits mobility and stimulation. It is also the nature of pain. For example, on account of rajas, fire spread; wind blows; the mind becomes restless, etc.

ax. *Tamas*. Tamas is the principle of passivity and negativity in things. Its colour is black. Itis opposed to the Sattva guna because it is heavy, laziness, drowsiness. It produces ignorance and darkness and leads to confusion and bewilderment.

Sattva, Rajas, and Tamas contradict as well as cooperate among each other to produce an object. These three gunas are present in all the objects of the world. None of them exist alone. Among them each guna tries to dominate the other two. Hence, they can't exist in a tranquility state. As a result, they can't remain pure for a single moment. Since they are changing continuously, distortion is their nature. There are two types of transformations occur in the gunas. These are, 'svarupa' and 'virupa'.

Svarupa. During pralaya or dissolution of the world, the gunas are changing within themselves without disturbing the others. That is, Sattva changes into Sattva, rajas changes into rajas and tamaj changes into tamaj. Such transformation of the gunas is called 'svarupaparināma' or change into the homogenous. In this stage, the gunas can neither create nor produce anything.

Virupa. In case of pralaya or dissolution of the world the gunas are in a state of constant flux and each tries to dominate the others. It is this flux of gunas that results in the formation of various objects. This kind of transformation is called virupa transformation or change into the heterogeneous. So, it is the starting point of the world's evolution.

Purusa. According to the Sāṁkhya Philosophy, Purusa or self is an eternal reality. Purusa is the self, subject and knower. It never be an object because, the existence of objects can be proved in some ways whereas, non-existence can't be proved in anyways. Purusa is neither the body, nor the mind (mānas), neither ego (ahaṁkāara) nor intellect (buddhi). It is not the substance which has the quality of consciousness. It is itself pure-consciousness. It is the basis of all knowledge and is the supreme knower. It can't be the object of knowledge. It is the observer, eternally free, the impartial spectator and peaceful. It is beyond the space-time continuum, change, and activity. It is the self enlightened, self-proved and hence, causasui. It is all pervading, formless, and eternal. Its existence can't be doubted because in its absence, all knowledge even doubt is not possible. It has been described as, devoid of three gunas, negative, inactive, solitary witness, observer, knower and of the nature of illumination. According to Sāṁkhya Philosophy, the purusa is of the nature of pure consciousness and hence beyond the limits of Prakṛti . It is free from distortions. It's objects changes but it itself never changes. It is above self-arrogance, aversion and attachment.

There are five arguments Sāṁkhya has given for establishing the existence of purusa. These are as follows;

- All the worldly objects are meant for some one. This is so because the conscious Prakṛti can't make use of them. Hence, all these substances are for Purusa or self. Prakṛti evolves itself in order to serve the Purusa's end. The three gunas, Prakṛti , and the subtle body, all are served to the Purusa.
- Purusa is a pure consciousness which is beyond our experience and analysis. It is the substratum of all knowledge both positive and negative. There can be no experience without him. This is so because he is the sole authority of all experiential knowledge.
- Since Prakṛti is unconscious, it can't enjoy her creation. Hence, a conscious element is needed to make use of them. Prakṛti is the one to be enjoyed (bhogyā) and so there must be an enjoyer (bhoktā). This argument supports the existence of Purusa.
- Substances of the universe are composed of three gunas. The purusa is the witness of three gunas and he is beyond from these gunas.
- There are persons who try to get relieved from all sorts of sufferings of the world. The desire for liberation and emancipation implies the existence of a person who can try for and obtain liberation. Hence, it is enforced to accept the existence of Purusa.

On the account of Sāṁkhya, there are pluralities of self or purusa. All these Purusas are identical in their essences and they are embedded with consciousness. Hence, consciousness is found in all the selves. This view is similar to Jainism and Mimansa because they believe in the plurality of selves.

Evolution. The world and worldly objects are created because of the contact between Prakṛti and Purusa. The Prakṛti alone can't create the world because it is material. In the same manner the Purusa can't create the world independently because he is inactive. Hence, the contact between Prakṛti and Purusa is necessary for the evolution to start though they are possessing different and opposite natures. An example can help you to understand the nature of Purusa and Prakṛti in a better way and clear manner. The Prakṛti is like a blind man and the Purusa is like a lame man cooperate each other to reach their destination. The lame man sits on the shoulders of the blind mind and pointing to him the way where to go and in which direction to move. In much the same manner, the inactive-eternal Purusa and the conscious Prakṛti cooperate with each other in order to start the evolution. Regarding their contact, the Sāṁkhya says, there is no real contact took place between Prakṛti and Purusa. But their mere closeness or nearness with each other disturbs the stability of the gunas of Prakrti. When these three gunas; sattva, rajas, tamas disturb and disrupt, they are constantly mixing and dissociating. As a consequence, evolution begins. A sage named Kapila has described the order of creation which is accepted by the Sāṁkhya Philosophy. The order of creation is as follows.

- **Mahat.** Mahat is the first product of evolution. It is cosmic in its nature. Besides this fact, it has psychological aspect in which it is called intellect or buddhi. Here, it is important to mention that buddhi should not be understood as the same as consciousness. The reason is buddhi is material whereas consciousness is eternal. An important function of buddhi is to take decision which is a part of memory act. This helps to distinguish between the known and the knower. Sattva is predominately found as an attribute of buddhi. Buddhi helps to identify the soul or the ātman which differs from all physical objects and their qualities.

- **Ahaṁkāra.** Ahaṁkāra is understood as 'ego' in English. It is the second product of evolution. Ego is identified as "I" or "mine" feelings of an individual. Every individual has buddhi, and since Ahaṁkāra is a practical element of buddhi, it is found in all individuals. Because of ego the purusa looks upon himself as an active agent, desire and strive for ends, and possesses characteristics. An individual perceives an object through sense organs. Then mind reflects on these perceptions and determines their nature. Following this, the attitude of 'mine' and 'for me' is attributed to these objects. This is nothing but regarded as 'ego'. In this product (Ahaṁkāra), all these three gunas of prakruti operates.

- **Mānas.** According to the Sāṁkhya Philosophy, mānas or mind is neither eternal nor atomic. It is constituted with parts and thus can come into contact with the different sense organs simultaneously. Mind helps to analyze and synthesize the sense-data into determinate perceptions. Being an internal sense organ, it is aware of objects belonging to the past, present, and the future.

- **Jñānendriyas.** Jñānendriyas are known as five sense organs; nose, ears, eyes, skin, and tongue. On Sāṃkhya views, sense is an imperceptible energy or force which exists in the perceived organs and apprehends the object. This implies, the sense is not the ears but their power of hearing. Thus, the senses are not perceptible but can infer. They are informed from the functions that they perform. The five sense organs produce knowledge of touch, colour, smell, heard, and taste. All these are born because of the Purusa and they are the result of ego or Ahaṃkāra.
- **Karmendriyas.** Karmendriyas is understood as the five organs of action which reside in mouth, ears, feet, anus, and the sex organ. They perform the functions respectively as speech, hearing, movement, excretion, and reproduction. The cause of the creation of these organs is the desire of Purusa for his experience.
- **Tanmātrās.** There are five tanmātr ās; sabda or sound, sparsa or touch, rupa or form, rasa or taste, and gandha or smell. All are very subtle because they are the elements of the objects. Hence, they can't be perceived but inferred. The Sāṃkhya School viewed that the five elements; earth, water, air, fire, and ether have their origin in the five tanmātrās.
- **Mahābhutas.** There are five mahabhutas found in the cosmos namely;Air or Vāyu, Fire or Agni, Akāsa or Ether, Water or Jala and Prathivi or Earth.

Their respective qualities are; touch, colour, sound, taste, and smell. The Sāmkhya theory of evolution is illustrated in the following diagram for your clarity and better understanding.

Epistemology

The Sāṃkhya philosophy recognizes three independent sources of valid knowledge (Pramā na). These are; perception, inference, and verbal testimony (sabda). According to the Sāṃkhya, self possess knowledge. To have knowledge of an object there should be contact between object and sense organs. Again, the connection must found between mind and sense organs. Lastly, mind is related to mahat for cognition. Thus the mahat becomes transformed into the form of particular objects. Mahat being unconscious and physical entity can't generate knowledge alone. Hence, it requires a conscious and eternal entity like Purusa. Since Purusa is pure consciousness helps Prakrti to generate knowledge. The Sāṁkhya Philosophy accepts two sorts of perception, savikalpaka and nirvikalpaka as Nyaya advocates. For detail discussion on savikalka and nirvikalpaka, please go to the Unit-1: Nyāya Philosophy. Without deviating from Nyaya Philosophy, the Sāṁkhya holds that vyāpti is found in all sorts of inference. For them, inference are of two sorts; i) affirmative (vita), ii) negative (avita). In case of the former, inferences are constituted of universal affirmative propositions. But in case of the later, it consists of universal negative propositions. The analysis of universal affirmative proposition and universal negative preposition are discussed in the Block. The Sāṁkhya accepts the five-membered syllogism of the Nyaya as the most adequate pattern of inference. The Sāṁkhya School adores sabda as an independent source of valid knowledge. Sabda or verbal testimony is of two kinds, 'laukika' and 'vaidika'. The analysis of laukika and vaidika are found in Nyaya Philosophy of this Block.

Bondage and Liberation

The self, who is eternal, pure conscious, and all pervading, due to its ignorance, identifies itself with the mānas, ahṁkara, and mahat which are the products of Prakrti. Thus, it experiences the worldly pain and suffering. The universe is constituted of manifold objects, and since objects are embedded with gunas and selves and even interrelated among them, suffering is unavoidable. This is so because the Sāṁkhya claims that wherever there is guna there is suffering. Further, they said that the life in heaven is also controlled by the gunas. Since there are sufferings and bondage, there are also paths leads to liberation, emancipation or salvation. On Sāṁkhya account, there are two sorts of liberation. These are Jivanmukti and Videhamukti. The self attains freedom from worldly suffering and realizes truth in one's life living in the earth is known as jivanmukti. In case of videhamukti, the self attains complete liberation from all sorts of sufferings. This is achieved after death only. Thus, videhamukti is known as kaivalya. This is understood as liberation from the gross body. The Sāṁkhya theory of liberation is termed as 'apavarga', the purusartha or the summum bonum of life.

Educational Implication of Samkhya Philosophy

The meaning of true Education: According to Samkhya Philosophy true Education is that Which acquaints one with the differences between Prakriti and Purush (matter and sprit). According to the principles of Samkhya philosophy and action (karya) is already inhererent in a cause, so it is a truism to remark that the development of man is already inherent in him (man).

The fundamental Purpose of Education: According to Samkhya 'Mukti' (or detiverance or liberation of the soul) is the ultimate purpose of one's life. This 'mukti' may be obtained through releasing the difference between the prakriti and purush (Matter and spirit). Therefore, the development of man should be so guided that he may distinguish between matter and sprit, and may obtain freedom from the miseries of life. According to Samkhya philosophy this is the end (Saddhya) or basic purpose of education. For the realization of this end the practice of yoga is necessary.

The Fundamental Aims of Education:

ax. The physical Development: That is full development of the senses and organs of action.

ax. The mental development: Full development of the mind in such a way as to make the ideas coming from it indicative of positive actions.

ax. The emotional development: To develop such a self-consciousness in which the Satva (righteousness) predominates.

ax. The intellectual Development: The development of intellect (Buddhi), to make it free of the slavery of senses and to involve it in the experience of the spirit (Purush)

ax. The moral Development: For this development it is necessary that the individual does not indulge in speaking lies, in violence, in stealing the individual has to be instructed to follow the austerity of satya, Ahimsa, Asteya, Aparigraha and Bradmacharya.

The concept of the curriculum according to Samkhya philosophy: The curriculum is a means for achieving the aim of education Samkhya philosophy admits the importance of both physical and spiritual aspects of life. Therefore, the curriculum should provide scope for the development of knowledge and activities pertaining to material and spiritual realms of life according to the various stages of development of an individual. According to Samkhya philosophy all types of subjects should be included in the curriculum and each should be taught according to students interests and aptitudes. Samkhya believes that and individual is ever-growing.

The Method of Teaching: According to Samkhya there are two principle means for acquiring knowledge. These are external and internal. Under the external means sense and organs of actions may be included. Under the internal one's come mind, self consciousness (Aham or Ahamkar) intellect and soul (Purush).

To Sankhya there are three means of acquiring knowledge:

1) Through the senses (Prataksha), 2) Interence (anuman) and 3) the statement of some authority or Vedas. 1) The pratyaksha Vidhi, 2) the Anuman Vidhi, 3) Shabda Vidhi.

Discipline (Anushashan): Sankhya Philosophy accepts the concepts of discipline as advocated by the yoga philosophy. 'Yama' and 'Niyam' are the first two principles of discipline according to yoga philosophy. The term 'Yam' means control (Sanyam) of thought, speech and deed (Manasa, Vacha and Karmana), For this control, the Yoga recommends observance of truth speaking, practice of non-violence, non-stealing, non-accumulating of wealth and observance of confinence. Niyam is the second aspect of discipline according to Yoga. Yoga recommends five Niyams ordisciplines cleanliness (Shauch), Contentment (Santosh) penance (Tap), Self-study (Swadhy aya) and dedicating everything to 'God' and being always rapt into his meditation (Pranayam)

The teacher: According to the Samkhya philosophy teacher should be a trust worthy and ideal person. He should have a vivid knowledge about the distinction between the matter and spirit (Prakriti and purush) Such a teacher alone can develop true knowledge in this students.

The students: The Sankhya Anekatmabadi Darshan, that is, this philosophy believes in many souls. There is no 'one soul' but many. Each one's soul has its own entity. Samkhya philosophy respects the personality of each student. Each individual has the three attributes of satva, Raj and Tam. Accordingly Samkhya philosophy enjoins each student to be disciplined and behave morally.

The School: During the developmental days of Samkhya philosophy the Gurukuls were working as seats of learning. In these Gurukuls individual teaching as is vogue. There was no group teaching, except group discussion in an assembly of learned person at occasions.

Conclusion

The Sāṁkhya philosophy is the oldest school among all the schools of Indian Philosophy. A sage named kapila was the founder of this school.

This system is dualistic because it accepts two ultimate realities, Purusa and Prakṛti . It advocates satkāryavāda, which expresses effect exists in its material cause prior to its production. On the account of Samkhya, Prakṛti - It is eternal, unconscious, and active. Purusa- It is eternal, pure conscious, and inactive. There are three gunas found in Prakṛti . These are sattva, rajas, and tamas. Nearness between Prakṛti and Purusa causes evolution. The order of creation is as follows: Mahat, ahamkāra, Mānas, Five sense organs (jnānendriyas), five organs of action (karmendriyas), Five subtle elements (tanmantrās) and Five physical elements. (mahābhutas). The Sāṁkhya philosophy believes there are three independent sources of valid knowledge. These are; perception, inference, and verbal testimony. According to the Sāṁkhya school of thought, bondage is due to the attachment towards worldly objects and liberation is the dissociation from worldly suffering and pain. On Sāṁkhya views, liberation is of two types as Jivanmukti and Videhemukti. One can attain jivanmukti while living in the earth and possessing physical body whereas, videhamukti is attained only after death. Thus, videhamukti is known as kaivalya or the summum bonum of life. Guna: Guṇa means 'string' or 'a single thread or strand of a cord.' In more abstract uses, it may mean 'a subdivision, species, kind, quality,' or an operational principle or tendency. Evolution: Evolution, in biology, is change in the genetic material of a population of organismsthrough successive generations. Although the changes produced in a single generation are normally small, the accumulation of these differences over time can cause substantial changes in a population, a process that can result in the emergence of new species. Samkhya's concepts of student, teacher, and discipline, through quite old, many even be accepted today as it is difficult to overlook the same if we want to strengthen our educational field. The Samkhya philosophy accepts the individual personality of man. Needless to remark that this concept appears to be at the root of modern democracy. Samkhya philosophy emphasises the development of all aspects of life.

CHAPTER SEVEN

CONTRIBUTION OF INDIAN EDUCATIONAL THINKERS

Introduction

It is worthless to mention that India has witnessed many eminent educational thinkers who have spared their entire life for the benefit of Nation. In this chapter, we shall study educational thoughts and some significant educational contributions of some prominent one. We will also explore the viewpoints of Indian thinkers on education. Against the backdrop of the growing discontent with western education in India, there is an impending need to understand how Indian thinkers have conceptualized the education system particularly in terms of its nature, extent, and scope. They represent indigenous thought with which both students and educators are able to relate. The purpose here is to look for viable alternatives that would play a transformative role in society and create a just and humane social order.

Rabindranath Tagore (1861 -1941)

Rabindranath Tagore was born in Kolkata to a deeply religious family of Landowners. His father Debendranath was a man of integrity, spiritual acumen, and strength of character. He cast a deep impact on Rabindranath in the formative years of life. Rabindranath Tagore was born on 7th May 1861. He completed his primary education from private tutors at his home and higher education at Saint Xavier C o l l e g e, Kolkata.

Definition of Education - Rabindranath Tagore has defined education as 'Education is Self-expression.'

He was awarded the Nobel prize for literature for his poetry ' G e e t a n j a l i ' Like many other children of aristocratic families of that time, the major part of Rabindranath's childhood was spent in servants' quarters under the care and authority of those who served his family. His first lessons were from the Bengali primer, Varna Parichaya. Later, he joined the Oriental Seminary, then the Normal School (which followed the teaching-learning pattern of English schools). He sought admission to the Bengali Academy in order to gain a grounding in English. He remained far from happy in school. The rooms were dismal, in fact, the entire building was unsuitable for human habitation. There were no pictures, not a stroke of colour, nothing that would motivate the students to attend school. Naturally, many of them played truant; those who did attend school regularly would remain filled with depression (Tagore 1966). The grim, monotonous, unhappy experience in school compelled him to consolidate his ideas on meaningful education and revolutionize the whole process of education. Tagore was opposed to the western system of education that emphasized learning from books with the sole objective of developing the intellectual potential of the child. He believed that education should be aimed not merely to develop the intellect but the complete personality of the child. An education Perspectives and Theories on Education system should cultivate and nurture among children the ability to learn directly from nature and life as such. Students should lead a simple, self-disciplined life based on the virtues of sociability, compassion, and the spirit of brotherhood. According to him, moral and spiritual values constituted the most important aspect of education.

Educational Contributions from Rabindranath Tagore

Shantiniketan School - Shantiniketan School was established in 1901, in Bolpur Village near Kolkata. Implementing his own educational thoughts was the objective behind establishment of this School. In Shantiniketan, classes had no walls and were conducted in open spaces. The teachers and pupils stayed together in the proximity of nature. Through common lunch and dinner, values of self-dependence and dignity of labour were nurtured. This school had subjects like gardening, book binding, carpentry, music, drama, dance, literature etc. Mother tongue was the medium of teaching and learning. In addition to mother tongue, additional languages such as English and Hindi were also used. There was in true sense a natural environment at the school.

Vishwabharati University - In 1921, Rabindranath Tagore converted Shanti Niketan School to Vishwabharati Vidyapeeth (University). The word Bharati in Vishwabharati means Sanskriti, i.e. culture. Hence, the University that creates global culture is Vishwabharati, is the meaning derived from this name. This is a well-known international university with the moto

'Yatra Vishvam Bhavati Ek Needam.' It means, 'where the world makes a home in a single nest.' This spirit is reflected in the name Vishwabharati.

Shriniketan - Rabindranath Tagore established Shriniketan in Surul village near Kolkata on 6th February 1922. 'Shri' in the name 'Shriniketan' means welfare or development. This is a vocational school and it focused on vocational and technical education. Sustainable development of people, community and environment by using local natural resources through education to rural people is the core objective of Shriniketan.

He criticized western education for treating the child as a receiver of packaged information in a way that did not awaken hislher own creativity and innate abilities. The children, in turn, pick up bits and pieces out of the information thrust upon them and present themselves for examination of their ability to retain the information. According to Tagore it was not enough to pass on information. What was important was the ability to put to use what one has learnt and to develop curiosity and alertness of mind. The child should be able to appreciate a sense of freedom acquired by ' free movements of the body in the midst of the natural environment. It may be understood at this stage itself that for Tagore, education stood for freedom from ignorance and from passion and prejudice. He upheld that the child learns the first lessons on freedom from nature which is the basic source of knowledge. According to Tagore, the ideal school should be established in the midst of fields, trees, and plants, under the open sky and far removed from human settlements. This would keep the children away from the turmoil's of daily life. More importantly living in the forest was associated with austere pursuits and renunciation. From his ideas, Tagore set out to develop an appropriate system of national education for India. He wanted to set up a school based on his ideals for which he travelled far and wide.Tagore settled at Santiniketan where he founded the Brahamacharya Ashram with only five students.The emphasis here was on a personalized relationship between teachers and pupils. Tagore himself taught English in the Ashram School. He would narrate stories from Indian history in the evening to the children. Having prepared the ground for school education, he diverted attention to higher education and established the Visva Bharati.

Swami Vivekananda (1863 – 1902)

Swami Vivekananda was born on 12th January, 1863, in Kolkata. He completed his primary schooling at Metropolitan school, Kolkata and higher education at Presidency College, Kolkata. He died on 4th July 1902. Childhood name of Swami Vivekananda was Narendra. His father -

Vishwanath Dutt, was a practising lawyer at Kolkata High Court. His mother Bhuvaneshwaridevi was religious by nature. The religious atmosphere at home had a great impact on the life of Swami Vivekananda. Since his childhood, Swami Vivekananda was bright and talented. He got obsessed with philosophy. After knowing about his interest in philosophy, Principal Rev. Hasty led him to Ramakrishna Paramhamsa. In 1881, he met Ramakrishna Paramhamsa. Quest for experiencing divine power led him to ask the question to Ramakrishna Paramhamsa, 'Have you seen the God?' Ramakrishna Paramathamsa clearly responded with confidence, 'Yes, I have seen Him. I shall of transformation in the life of Vivekananda. He became a disciple of Ramakrishna Paramahamsa.

Definition of Education - According to Swami Vivekananda, "Education is the manifestation of the perfection already within man."

Meeting his Guru and accepting Sanyas by Swami Vivekananda

Dr. Ramchandra Dutt, a relative of Narendra who had been raised in his house was a disciple of Shri Ramkrishna Paramhansa. He noticed that Narendra was inspired by religious feelings to such an extent that he was contemplating renunciation in his childhood itself. He once told Narendra, "Brother, if your only goal in life is to further the enhancement of our religion, then do not get involved in the Bramho Samaj or others. You go to Dakshineshwari and meet Shri Ramkrishna." Narendra met Shri Ramkrishna at his neighbor Surendranath's house itself. Initially for some days Shri Ramkrishna did not allow Narendranath to leave his side even for a moment. He made Narendra sit next to him and gave him much advice & counsel. The two of them would have great discussions when alone.

Shri Ramkrishna had decided to give Narendra the responsibility of carrying on his incomplete mission. One day Shri Ramkrishna wrote on a piece of paper, "Narendra will perform the task of enlightening the masses." Somewhat hesitantly Narendranath replied, "I won't be able to do all this." Shri Ramkrishna immediately spoke with great resolve, "What? Won't be able? Your bones will perform this task?" Later Shri Ramkrishna initiated Narendranath on the path of Sanyas and gave him the name Swami Vivekanand.

Establishment of Ramkrishna Mission by Swami Vivekananda

Swami Vivekananda along with Taraknath, another disciple of Ramkrishna, established the Ramkrishna Mission after Mahasamadhi of Shri Ramkrishna Paramhansa. It began its activities from a dilapidated building at Varahnagar, near Kolkata. Earlier it was believed that this place was a haunted house. Vivekanandakept Shri Ramkrishna's mortal ashes and some other objects used by him, at this place. Soon Shri Ramkrishna's disciples started living there.

Importance of Swami Vivekananda

Swami Vivekananda putting curb on conversions with his stormy propagation of 'Vedanta' in other countries. India was ruled by the British during the period of Swami Vivekananda. Owing to the influence of British education system, their culture, strategies of Christian missionaries misleading people and their literature, the affluent class in Bharat developed inferiority complex feeling that Hindu Dharma and culture is of very low standard, inhuman and barbarian. Many Hindus would have been baptized and adopted Christianity; but there is no doubt that it was curbed due to the fiery propagation of 'Vedanta' in other countries by Swami Vivekananda. Swami Vivekananda gave message of spiritual unison and creating new consciousness amongst youth. Swami Vivekananda represented India and consequently, Hindu Dharma in a world conference was held in Chicago for all religions in the year of 1893. Swami Vivekananda gave a message of spiritual unity to the world in this conference. He also emphasized that along with spiritual progress, materialistic / worldly progress was equally important. Swami Vivekananda's guidance helped to generate new consciousness and enthusiasm amongst the youth. Swami Vivekananda's enlightening guidance on education system. Education should be such that it would create 'human' and character. The burden of knowledge not understood throughout life but somehow filled in the brains does not mean Education. Education should be such that it will create 'human', good character inculcating good thoughts.

Mohandas Karamchand Gandhi (1869 – 1948)

Mohandas Karamchand Gandhi was born in Porbandar situated in Kathiawar, Gujarat. His father and grandfather were chief ministers in Kathiawar. After completing school education he went to London to study law. He came back to the country and practised law in Mumbai and Rajkot. He did not get much success in the profession and went to South Africa on an unexpected offer. His experiments in education started when he returned to South Africa in 1897 with his two sons and a nephew for whom he searched for an appropriate school. He could have sent them to the school for European children but did not think that English as a medium of instruction employed in those schools was worthwhile. He used to run the 'Tolstoy Farm' which could not afford to pay the wages that qualified teachers would demand. So; he took upon himself the task of teaching the children. He decided to live among the children and lay the foundation of character-building and self-dependence in them. Gandhi encouraged the children to undertake all the chores ranging from cooking to scavenging themselves. Certainly, a teacher would cooperate and guide them throughout the endeavour. Apart from physical training he engaged in spiritual training of students (Prasad 2001). He returned to India in 1914 where he was destined to play a major role in the freedom struggle and importantly, in the educational reconstruction of the country.

Definition of Education: According to Mahatma Gandhi, "Literacy is not the end of education, not even the beginning. By education, I mean, drawing out of the best in man's body, mind and spirit."

"By education I mean an all-round drawing out of the best in child and man-body, mind and spirit. Literacy is not the end of education or even the beginning." - M.K. Gandhi

Gandhi was concerned with the rising trend of people giving up their vocation Theories on Education after acquiring western education. Cobblers, carpenters, blacksmiths, masons, tailors tended to surrender their vocations treating them as inferior. They would take pride in joining the position of clerk in offices.

His philosophy of education is a harmonious blending of Idealism, Naturalism and Pragmatism. Idealism is the base of Gandhi's philosophy whereas Naturalism and Pragmatism are the helpers in translating that philosophy into practice. Therefore he is known as practical- idealist. His nation was "...education for life, education through life, and education throughout life." This definition of Mahatma Gandhi would comprise everything that can be conceived under education. Gandhi's Educational thought which were influenced by his philosophy of life are the following:

- According to Gandhi, schools should be self-sufficient so that the poorest of the poor could educate themselves. This could happen only if the schools could generate enough resources for themselves. Further, schools that are self-sufficient do not fall prey to the whims and interference of the state. Teachers should not be made to give in to the dictates of bureaucracy and teach out of the curriculum laid down by it. Learning was not confined to memorizing contents in the textbooks.
- Gandhi believed that in India where more than 80 per cent of the population subsists by agriculture and about 10 per cent by industries,

delimiting the scope of education to literacy was not appropriate. Boys and girls should be encouraged to value manual labour. In fact, carpentry, spinning and other crafts may be used as a means of stimulating the intellect.

- This can be made possible by explaining the underlying mechanism. When a child interested in spinning, for instance, is explained the mechanism of the working of the wheel, the history of cotton, the method of determining the strength of the yarn, his/her intellect gets sharpened. This was true education.
- He was in favour of the mother tongue as the medium of instruction, for English creates a divide between those who are 'highly educated' and the many uneducated people.
- Moreover, comprehension is faster and better when children are taught in their mother tongue. Gandhi clearly stated that if English were removed from the curriculum of primary and secondary or high school education then it would be possible to make the children go through the whole course in seven years instead of eleven years.

Mahatma Gandhi is a spirit of profound wisdom and captivating humility, armed with only an iron will and inflexible resolve and a frail man who confronted the brutality of military strength with the dignity of a simple human being. He believed in God implicitly. According to him, though individuals have different bodies, yet the same soul pervades in all of us. In short, Gandhiji experienced and realized Unity in Diversity. His philosophy of life has four elements namely- (1) Truth, (2) Non-Violence (3) Fearlessness and (4) Satyagraha

Gandhiji's philosophy to life is based upon the philosophy of Idealism. He advocated the ideals of truth, non-violence and moral values to achieve the ultimate truth of self-realization. He is child according to his nature and he becomes a pragmatist when he advocates learning by doing and learning by experience. All these lead to an integration, so essential to effective education and development of the total personality.

Gandhi's Educational Thoughts

Gandhiji's Basic Education was the practical embodiment of his philosophy of education. His basic education takes up the challenging task of preparing the young learners to become morally sound, individually independents, socially constructive, economically productive and responsible future citizens which can prove helpful in solving the problem of unemployment by making youth self-employed by giving them skill training. Gandhiji believed that education should develop all the capacities of the child so that he becomes a complete human being. In this way, fully and harmoniously developed personality is able to realize the ultimate aim of life which is Truth or God. Gandhiji has himself explained - "By education I mean all-round drawing out of the best in child's and man's body, mind and spirit. Literacy is neither the beginning nor the end of education. This is only a means through which man or woman can be educated." His Basic Principles of Education includes:

ax. From seven to fourteen years of age, education of each child should be free, compulsory and universal.

ax. The medium of instruction should be mother-tongue.

ax. Mere literacy cannot be equated with education. Education should employ some craft as a medium of education so that the child gains economic self-reliance for his life.

ax. Education should develop human values in the child.

ax. Education should create useful, responsible and dynamic citizens. By education all the hidden powers of child should develop according to the community of which he is an integral part.

ax. Education should achieve the harmonious development of child's body, mind, heart and soul.

ax. All education should be imparted through some productive craft or industry and a useful correlation should be established with that industry. The industry should be such that the child is able to achieve gainful work experience through practical work.

ax. Education should be made self-supporting through some productive work. Education should lead to economic independence and self-reliance for livelihood.

Thus, in Gandhiji's educational thoughts the development of the personality of child is more important than mere literacy or knowledge of different subjects. In other words he believed in life-centered as well as child-centered education. Besides learning of three R's Reading, Writing and Arithmetic in school, he insisted on development of these H's Hand, Heart and Head. Thus, the aim of Education should be of developing the integrated personality of the child.

Sri Aurobindo (1872 – 1950)

Sri Aurobindo, original name **Aurobindo Ghose**, Aurobindo also spelled **Aravinda**, Sri also spelled **Shri**, (born August 15, 1872, Calcutta [now Kolkata], India—died December 5, 1950, Pondicherry [now Puducherry]), yogi, seer, philosopher, poet, and Indian nationalist who propounded a philosophy of divine life on earth through spiritual evolution.

Aurobindo's education began in a Christian convent school in Darjeeling (Darjiling). While still a boy, he was sent to England for further schooling. He entered the University of Cambridge, where he became proficient in two classical and several modern European languages. After returning to India in 1892, he held various administrative and professorial posts in Baroda (Vadodara) and Calcutta (Kolkata). Turning to his native culture, he began the serious study of Yoga and Indian languages, including classical Sanskrit.

According to Sri Aurobindo, any system of education should be founded on the study of the human mind. The reason is simple: while the material with which artists deal is inert, that of educators and educationists is highly sensitive.

- The major defect in the European system of education is precisely its insufficient knowledge of psychology. The means through which education could be made meaningful was to acquire an understanding of the instruments of knowledge and develop a system of teaching which was natural, easy, and effective, The teachers need to accept their role as that of a helper and guide not as an instructor who imparts knowledge, trains the mind of the children, and makes impositions on them.

- At best, the teacher can make suggestions and encourage the children to acquire knowledge for themselves. Admittedly, children of younger age need greater help and guidance than older children. The children should be given the freedom to choose their own qualities, virtues, capacities, capabilities, and career.

- It is improper to impose one's ideas on them. Education needs to be geared to drawing out the innate abilities in children and perfecting them for noble use.

- Furthermore, the children should be made familiar and aware of all that surrounds them and which meets them on a day-to-day basis, e.g., natural-physical environment, sounds, habits and customs, nationality. The purpose here is to foster free and natural growth, for these are the prerequisites of genuine development.

- He believed that the mother-tongue served as the appropriate medium of instruction. Children should acquire competence in the medium first not by making them spell words, read books but by familiarizing them with interesting parts of literature.

- A Large part of their study should be devoted to the development of mental faculties and moral character. The foundation for the study and appreciation of art history, philosophy and science could be laid at this stage itself. Often, the idea of universal education is pursued as a mission with complete disregard of what education is or what it should ideally be.

Aurobindo's voluminous literary output comprises philosophical speculation, many treatises on yoga and integral yoga, poetry, plays, and other writings. In addition to *The Life Divine*, his major works include *Essays on the Gita* (1922), *Collected Poems and Plays* (1942), *The Synthesis of Yoga* (1948), *The Human Cycle* (1949), *The Ideal of Human Unity* (1949), *Savitri: A Legend and a Symbol* (1950), and *On the Veda* (1956).

Sarvepalli Radhakrishnan (1888 - 1975)

Sarvepalli Radhakrishnan was born in Tiruttani near Chennai. He specialized in the understanding of the ethics of Vedanta. In fact, he upheld that one way to get to the very core to culture in India is by acquiring knowledge of Sanskrit or any other indigenous language by whatever means is natural and stimulating to the mind. When this happens, it would be possible to establish continuity between the still living power of our past and the yet uncreated power of our future, and how we are to learn and use English or any other foreign language so as to know helpfully the life, ideas and culture of other countries and establish own right relations with the world around us" (ibid, pp. 209). This is the aim of national education.wrote a dissertation on the ethics of the Vedanta and its metaphysical presuppositions. His interest and study of Indian philosophy developed a great deal after he was offered a position in the Department of Philosophy at the Madras Presidency College following which he joined as Professor of Philosophy at the University of Mysore.

Definition of Education: According to Dr. Radhakrishnan, education is not mere literacy. Education must create human beings. It must include not only the training of the intellect but the refinement of the heart and the disciplined spirit.

Radhakrishnan was subsequently appointed to the King George V Chair of Mental and Moral Science in the University of Calcutta. Later, representing India, he addressed the Philosophical Congress at Harvard University. He was invited to join the Manchester College, Oxford. He severed as Spalding Professor of Eastern Religions and Ethics at Oxford University and Fellow of the British Academy. Back in India, he remained Vice Chancellor (between 1939 and 1948) of the Banaras Hindu University, Leader of lndian delegation to UNESCO (between 1946 and 1952), Ambassador of lndia to the USSR (between 1949 and 1952), Vice President of India (between 1952 and 1962), President, General Conference of UNESCO (between 1952 and 1954), Chancellor, University of Delhi (between 1953 and 1962), and President of lndia (between 1962 and 1967). Radhakrishnan believed that an education system should be geared to both train the intellect as also in-stilt grace in the heart and in doing so bring about balanced growth of an individual.

Educational thoughts of Dr. Sarvapalli Radhakrishnan

ax. Education for Humanity-Education must offer nurturance of empathy, kindness, trust, ethics, morality, harmony, collaboration, respect etc.

ax. Curriculum should Impart Comprehensive Knowledge about People, Society and Nature-Educational curriculum must include information and knowledge about the environment we live in, our nature, the characteristics and the needs of nature. It must also include the efforts we must take for addressing the needs of the nature and our environment.

ax. Education for Democracy-Education must nurture democratic values. Today's students have to be nurtured as responsible citizens of tomorrow, strong and able to lead our country. Hence democratic values must be inculcated through education.

ax. Development of Scientific Attitude - For developing India in 21st century and youth with scientific attitude, we must nurture scientific attitude through education.

ax. Education for Preservation, Enrichment and Transmission of Culture - Culture, that includes religion, traditions, customs, thoughts, social conduct etc. comes under a threat under the influence of western culture. Education must contribute to its preservation, enrichment and transmission. Students must be made aware of the values of our culture.

ax. Education for Self-discipline - Self-discipline is crucial for personality development. It has a potential to bring about everlasting transformation in our behaviour. Hence education must impart self-discipline.

ax. Women should get an Opportunity of Education and Self Development - Spiritual and cultural character of any society depends on the status of women of that society. Hence women education must be planned systematically for development of family, society and the nation.

ax. Education for Balanced Personality Development - Education must develop cognitive, emotional, constructive abilities of students for nurturing a responsible citizenship among them.

Educational contribution of Dr. Sarvapalli Radhakrishnan

Vice Chancellor- Dr. Sarvapalli Radhakrishnan was the Vice Chancellor of two important universities- Andhra University (1931-1938) and Banaras Hindu University (1939-1948). He set the benchmark of how to function as an efficient Vice Chancellor of a University. (3) Indian Ambassador, Vice President and President of India - Dr. Sarvapalli Radhakrishnan served as Indian Ambassador to Russia (1948), served twice as the Vice President of India (1952 - 1962) and served as the President of India (1962). He played a crucial role, working on these positions.

Chairman of University Education Commission- After independence, Government of India constituted University Education Commission in 1948, for educational transformation. Commission was assigned with the responsibility to offer guidelines for necessary transformation to higher education in India. Dr. Sarvapalli Radhakrishnan, as the Chairman of this commission played a crucial role.

Chanakya (4ᵗʰ century BCE)

The Maurya Empire, which Chanakya helped to establish, at its territorial height.

A Philosopher and statesman, Chanakya wrote the Arthashastra, an ancient text on political economy which has been compared favorably to the work of Machiavelli; as it focuses on keeping a ruler in power by means of wise rule and empowerment of the poor and not merely wicked statecraft. As an adviser to the emperor ChandraguptaMaurya, he was one of the chief architects of the MauryaEmpire, which would come to dominate the subcontinent for 150 years and would be led by the great Ashoka at its apex.

"If a king is energetic, his subjects will be equally energetic. If he is reckless, they will not only be reckless likewise, but also eat into his works.

Besides, a reckless king will easily fall into the hands of his enemies. Hence the king shall ever be wakeful."

Seven Sutras of Chanakya on Education and Students

ax. Acharya Chanakya is golden milestone in the making of our nation and is respected throughout the world. He is regarded as one of the most remarkable people whose versatililty ranged from being a great sage, Philosopher, Educationist, Administrator, strategist to a sharp Economist. In the book Chanakya Niti, he put forth aphorisms for leading a successful life– a code of conduct on topics like Education, Knowledge, Wisdom, Religion, Guru Shishya, Parents, values etc.

ax. Acharya Chanakya conveys to students that if they wish to seek true education then they must shun these Eight activities: all pleasures that tempt sense; tastes that gratify the tongue; anger and greed, personal beautification, too much entertainment, excessive sleeping and extreme indulgence in anything.

ax. Stressing further he adds that if one wishes for comfort then he should drop the idea of studying and at the same if anyone wants to study sincerely then he should stop craving for comfort. One can never indulge in comfort and education both at the same time.

ax. Chanakya says an uneducated man no matter how good he may look or to what family he may belong; he is as useless as the flower that has color but no fragrance. He says status of family and physical beauty add no significance to one's personality and they should never be rested upon. Only education attributes strength, character, knowledge and virtues to one's personality.

ax. Chanakya metaphorically compares Knowledge to a cow and says that just as a mother protects her child in the same way knowledge saves a person in difficult situations. Even in the most adverse times a knowledgeable person through his wisdom can handle all and carve out a way for himself.

ax. According to Chanakya, An uneducated person is useless and a scholar belonging to a lowly rated or renowned family is adored by all including God. Here we can understand that Acharya has tried to convey that we should never discriminate among various castes and classes. A person's credibility and worth should only be judged from his actions that are a display of his wisdom and education.

ax. Chanakya says a man devoid of wealth is not a 'poor man but the one who is devoid of education is actually a pauper in all aspects as his soul is empty of virtues. Therefore, such a man in real sense lives a beggar's life

Importance of Education

The learned Acharya says that as we gather each drop of water while filling the pitcher/pot the same way we must accumulate more and more knowledge, faith/dharma and wealth too. In the long term this builds into a massive treasure which benefits us all through life.

Chanakya Quotes about Education

- Education is the best friend. An educated person is respected everywhere. Education beats the beauty and the youth.
- The wise man should restrain his senses like the crane and accomplish his purpose with due knowledge of his place, time and ability.
- He who is overly attached to his family members experiences fear and sorrow, for the root of all grief is attachment. Thus one should discard attachment to be happy.
- Books are as useful to a stupid person as a mirror is useful to a blind person.
- There is some self-interest behind every friendship. There is no friendship without self-interests. This is a bitter truth.

Chanakya's contribution as an Administrator, Educationist, Strategist and Economist created a big stir around the world. His norms, strategies and principles are valid and followed even today. At present there is no dearth of chaos around the world and inside us, if we follow even a few of his sutras they can shape us into strong charactered individuals and steer us successfully through life.

Conclusion

We have come to realize that Indian thinkers on education weave strands from philosophy and pragmatism together as warp and woof. According to them, the scope of education extends beyond letters and words to encompass the totality of being. Meaningful education, they laid down, is preparation for life, for meeting challenges squarely, and for self-enrichment. Education is freedom from fear and ignorance leading to liberation. In this sense it is both the means as also the ultimate objective of life.

MAHATMA GANDHI AND HIS PHILOSOPHY

Introduction

The teachings of Mahatma Gandhi are famous worldwide, and they revolve around the concepts of ahimsa (non-violence), satyagraha, and self-reliance. He is called the Father of the Nation since he carried the freedom movement on his shoulders and ensured that India became independent. Gandhi's Educational Philosophy is a shining beacon for students; laying down the path they can follow to become the greatest minds of the century. It can teach us how to change the world and make it a better and egalitarian place. Given below are some essays that students can refer to. Mahatma Gandhi believed that education was among the most critical facets of the functioning of the personality as well as society and the world overall. A nation with educated young people can evolve at a much faster pace than a country with an ignorant population. He claimed that every child in India had to be trained as education was the secret to a successful life. Some of his ideologies were:

- **Free Compulsory Education:** Gandhiji wished to provide free, mandatory, and standardized primary education at the age of 7 and 14.
- **Craft-oriented teaching:** Gandhiji presumed that the highest advancement of body and spirit was possible only by handicrafts. He believed that self-sustenance could be obtained by learning the mechanical jobs involved in handicraft production.
- **Self-sustenance:** Gandhiji believed that the matter of primary education for the masses could not be delayed, even for a minute. The central

education system cannot be discontinued for lack of resources. Students could not wait until the ruling party had organized the required funds. He also stated that schooling would be self-sustaining.

- **Mother Tongue as the means of instruction:** One of the apparent shortcomings of the current school program was that schooling was provided by the use of a foreign language-English. It prevented the production of comprehension and accuracy of thinking or consistency of mind.
- **Concept of non-violence:** The extension of the idea of non-violence to the teaching of the infant as a prospective citizen of the world became a distinctive characteristic of Gandhiji's educational ideology. The universal education system (Buniyadi Shiksha) is imbued with the cardinal doctrine of non-violence and the principle of co-operative life.

Based on those universal values, Gandhian educational concepts do not sacrifice their fundamental importance in the years to come. The plans would have to conceive about a self-sustaining primary education that would change the condition of the community's lowest. The argument that schooling should be focused on experience, problem-solving and constructive practice rather than pure book study is entirely accurate.

Main Principles of Gandhi's Educational Philosophy:

1.All round development: As an absolute idealist, Gandhiji believed in the spiritual aims of education. By education he meant, "An all round drawing out of the best in child and man -body, mind and spirit." All round development – physical, mental, intellectual, aesthetic, moral and spiritual and not mere literary is the true goal of national education. "True education should result not in material power but in spiritual force.

"This was the ultimate aim. But he did not lose sight of the immediate aim of education, which is to impart training in citizenship, build character, give professional training and impart culture. for training in citizenship he wanted the pupils to know the functioning of Panchayats and local bodies and to practice democracy in schools."

2. Character building: He introduced craft in order to encourage dignity of labour, self-sufficiency and to break down the existing barriers of prejudices between the so- called intellectuals and the manual workers. Again he laid emphasis or character-building. He draws the corrective in the following words:

"All our learning of recitation of Vedas, correct knowledge of Sanskrit, Latin or Greek and what not, will avail us nothing, if they do not avail us to cultivate absolute purity of heart. The end of all knowledge's must be building of character." Again he says, "Students have to search within and to look after their personal character. Purity of personal life is an indispensable condition of building a sound education. The means to character building is not outer discipline or restraint from outside, but inner discipline or restraint from within. Self-restraint is a virtue and it conforms to the universal law. As he says, "Restraint self- imposed is no compulsion. A man who chooses the path of freedom from retrains releases himself. All things in the universe obey certain laws. It is discipline and restraint that separate us from the brute.

3. Self-sufficiency: Gandhiji was alive to the need of every individual. Hence he signalized economics self- sufficiency as one of the most important fruits of good education. He was painfully conscious of the fact that prevailing system of education caused educated unemployment and made the educated person helpless. He wanted the pupils to learn their native professions – agriculture and cottage industry. The craft bias to education would bring about economic prosperity and enable them to choose independent career, be self-sufficient and contribute to the society by acting as economic producers.

4. Cultural development: Again, the cultural aim of education was well-emphasised by Gandhiji. According to him, it is the function of education to impart culture and native heritage. This culture," he said "should show itself in smallest detail of your conduct and personal behaviour, now you sit, how you walk, how you dress, etc. Inner culture must be reflected, in your speech, the way in which you treat visitors and guests and behave towards one another and your teachers and elders. "Education must transmit the age old spiritual traditions of our land. Our pupils must not remain foreigners in their native land. They must be truly Indians. Gandhiji further says:

"The field of education which holds the seed of the future of the children to the soil requires absolute sincerity, fearlessness in the pursuit of truth and boldest experiment, provided always that they are sound and based upon deep thought, matured and sanctified by a life of consecration."

5. Social uplift and Welfare: The goal of national education according to Gandhiji is the same as the goal of the society explained above. Education must be based on social good, welfare for all, and must uplift the human aspect rather than the mechanistic aspect. The must build relationship between the material gain in the spiritual values. None of the two are to be ignored. National education must build our society, free from exploitation and class-distinction an ideal state (Ramarajya). These ideals must be put into actual practice in the school. Manual work and craft work will ensure dignity of labour. Charkha is an emblem of decentralization of industries. Community activities will foster co-operation and goodwill. Village pupils will continue their native profession. There will be no class distinction in the school. Education will be related to life.

Integral education, which allows the entire being of an individual to evolve, education that stresses character-building and cultural identification, is again obviously desirable. It is equally clear that, in our state-sponsored schemes, we have failed miserably to provide free, compulsory education to all. As a consequence, the Gandhian paradigm maintains its importance and appeal. Nevertheless, whether this knowledge may be learned exclusively or mainly by studying art, and if future recipients or the state approves it, remains to be seen. Finally, the Gandhian paradigm requires, in my view, an interconnected framework for integrating or addressing older and newest innovations that are evolving every day.

He incorporated the ideas of self-reliance and non-violence in his educational philosophy. Gandhi's understanding of creation, schooling, and society was modern. He utilized the three main philosophies of education in his writings. These were the concepts of naturalism, idealism, and pragmatism. His teachings will serve as a source of inspiration to students of future generations. Mahatma Gandhi's Educational Philosophy is given here in brief:

- His educational philosophy bloomed during his experiences as a lawyer in South Africa
- Gandhi's involvement in the freedom movement and the British's cruelty inspired him to write his educational philosophy
- His philosophy incorporates craft education schemes
- The philosophy is based on the values of non-violence
- Gandhi's teachings revolve around the concept of non-violence
- He tells us to be socially aware and help those in need around us
- Gandhi stresses the importance of learning and studying in our mother tongue
- He wants free and compulsory education for children between the ages of 7 to 14

- His view on education is a source of inspiration for students around the world
- If we follow his educational philosophy, we can make our country a wonderful place

The top six general philosophies of Mahatma Gandhi are:

1. Faith in God: He had a profound faith in God and believed in the unity of man. Like Froebel, he said, the ultimate reality in this universe is God. He is changeless that holds altogether, that creates, dissolves and recreates. According to him, "God is un-definable-a mysterious power that pervades everything. His presence is proved not by extraneous evidence but in the transformed conduct and character of those who have felt the real presence of God within."He, therefore, advised to have a living faith in a living God who is the ultimate arbiter of our fate. His will is supreme. "All life in its essence is one and that men are working consciously or unconsciously towards the realization of that identity." Therefore, he believed that the goal of life is to realize God.

2. Truth: Truth is the highest goal, and also it is the means to realize God. He does not demarcate a line of difference between truth and God. Until 1931 he said, "God is Truth" but thence he said, "Truth is God". He says, "I have no God to serve but Truth. Truth is expressed through the inner voice. It is the call of conscience. It should pervade the whole life. He believed in the practical application of truth in our daily behaviour and in our dealings with our fellow men. Truth is the guiding principle of human conduct. This truth is the ultimate reality which must triumph over evil and hatred." His advice was to realize that "Truth is life".

3. Non-Violence: The means to attain the goal of Truth is Ahimsa or Nonviolence. To him, "Ahimsa and Truth are so intertwined that it is practically impossible to disentangle and separate them." They are the two sides of a coin, or rather a smooth metallic disc, where it is not possible to say "which is the obverse and which is the reverse"? Ahimsa is not a negative attitude; it is a positive attitude of tolerance, patience, perseverance, self-sacrifice, self-suffering, humility, charity, forbearance, rise above attachment and hatred. A non-violent person must live a life of Tapasya or austere living. Non- violence is a great power which must be accepted as the law of life, must pervade the whole being and not be applied to isolated acts. It is not the weapon of the coward and weak but of the strongest to defeat the evil and malignant forces.

4. Love: He said that it is only through love that one can attain truth. To see the universal and all-prevailing spirit of truth face to face, one must be able to love the nearest of creation as oneself. One can conquer the enemies and brutal evil forces not by becoming evil but through love. Just as God is truth, God is also Love. We love and serve God when we love and serve His creatures.

God, said Gandhiji, "instead of being in the temple, church and Mosque, is to be found in the temple of humanity." His concept of Ram Rajya is truly the reflection of his concept of love, Ahimsa and Truth. These three cardinal values are identical in nature.

5. An Ideal Society: He dreamt a dream of ideal society which would be free from any form of exploitation, social differences, violence, hat redness and injustice. He aimed at to create a class-less society characterised by universal brotherhood, truth, freedom, love, justice and equality of all. Moral force and moral sanction would be the guiding principle of such a society. Each individual must be trained to be a useful citizen, shouldering the responsibility and fulfilling his/her duties. He is quite cynical to a society where wealth is a concentrated in a few hands. He conceded the right of everyone to keep as much for himself as was "necessary for a refined, civilized and moral life." Such society would secure the bare necessities of life and in such society women would be respected. In fact, the society has not a hypothetical thinking of Gandhiji. He gave his conception of future India in the following lines

"I shall work for an India in which the poorest shall feel that it is their country, in who making they have an effective voice, an India in which these shall be no high class or low class of people, an India in which all communities shall live in perfect harmony. There can be no room in such an India for the curse of untouchability or the curse of intoxicating drinks and drugs...women will enjoy the same rights as men...This is the India of my dream." Thus, a new social order will be built upon the pillars of morality, Ahimsa, love, harmony, equality, fraternity, and justice.

6. Satyagraha: It is the supreme principle which implies an adherence to truth in one's life. A seeker of truth can practice truth in his life in all its manifestations. A Satyagrahi is free from fear and learns to stick to truth whatever may come on his way. He is a lover of enemy and can conquer the evil forces by truth-a formidable weapon in his hand. Moreover he is not a coward, rather a brave, straight-forward and courageous.

Basic Education (Buniyadi Shiksha): Gandhi developed a system of education after 40 years of trials and experiments in order to bring his vision of society to life. His ideas changed the way people thought about education. Basic education, also known as Wardha education, or Nai Talim, or new education, or Buniyandi Shiksha, is a form of education. Gandhiji used the word "basic" to describe his educational scheme because it is so closely linked to Indian children's basic needs and desires. It is also closely linked to the people who live in the villages. It is a scheme to educate the common man, who is the foundation or backbone of our country. A Basic Education's aim is to allow a student to obtain the desired fruit through his or her own actions. Characteristics of Basic Education: Basic Education embodied Gandhi's vision of the ideal society as a set of small, self-sufficient societies.

The basic scheme of education has the following important features:

1. The primary goal of Basic Education is to assist students in being self-sufficient.
2. Manual labour was heavily emphasized in basic education.
3. Education should be free, compulsory, and universal for children aged 7 to 14.
4. It envisions providing education by craft or constructive work so that the child can become economically self-sufficient for the rest of his life. The medium of education should be the mother tongue.
5. Education should help children develop human values.
6. The aim is for the child's body, mind, heart, and soul to grow in a harmonious manner.
7. Education is imparted in a simple scheme by any local craft or useful job.
8. The cost of basic education is covered by productive jobs.
9. It is designed to produce people who are useful, responsible, and dynamic..

10. Craft, the world, and other subjects are all taught in conjunction with each other.

Gandhiji's contributions to Education

Gandhiji made a significant contribution to education. He was the first Indian to argue for an educational system focused on Indian culture and civilization's core values. The following are some of his significant contributions to education:

· Gandhiji proposed a comprehensive and realistic educational system tailored to our country's genius. It is a humane and positive framework that is based on national needs and values.

· He proposed a practical education plan focused on equality, social justice, nonviolence, human dignity, economic well-being, and cultural self-respect.

· Gandhiji described education as the all-around creation of a person's personality..

· He advocated for immediate and long-term educational goals that are in line with India's sociopolitical, fiscal, cultural, and social goals.

· He proposed a curriculum that was both realistic and broad in scope. An integrated, psychologically sound curriculum is needed.

· Gandhiji's proposed teaching approach is both logical and pedagogically sound..

· Gandhiji's educational model was not only comprehensive and realistic, but also highly decentralized and integrated, with a proven ability to inspire the whole society and place responsibility and accountability at the community level rather than at the state level.

·. The basic educational scheme was a viable solution to rural unemployment. Gandhiji was successful in providing a form of education that can provide the economic self-sufficiency and self-reliance that is needed.

Relevance of Gandhi's views on Education in the modern contest

The most critical aspect of Gandhi's educational scheme is the focus on connecting school education to societal needs. He hoped to accomplish this goal by employing a method of learning while receiving. He emphasized the importance of mastering the art. Job experience and socially meaningful positive work play an important role in today's school curriculum, as can be seen. His opinions on early childhood education are still valid today. The importance of parental education is emphasized for the proper development of children in their early years. Throughout the time, his focus on education through the mother tongue was widely accepted

Conclusion

Gandhiji made a significant contribution to education. He was the first Indian to argue for an educational system focused on Indian culture and civilization's core values. His methods and strategies, as well as the climate he recommended, revolutionized Indian thought and lifestyle. He was a true believer in idealism. He desired to put his thoughts and principles into action. His educational philosophy is a well-balanced mix of idealism, naturalism, and pragmatism. "Education is about bringing out the best in child and man-body, mind, and spirit," Gandhiji said. . He believed that literacy could never be the end or even the beginning of education. True education, he believes, is that which draws out and activates children's intellectual and physical abilities. He put a higher value on the child than on educational strategies and methods. He was a true believer that a good education could result in useful people for all of humanity. Education, in its real and general sense, is a lifelong process that starts at birth and continues indefinitely. Learning of computers, mobiles, and the internet along with the benefits of Artificial Intelligence has to be incorporated into such frameworks. As it stands, it tends to be quite backward-looking or, at any rate, built for a stagnant culture in which constant ancestral jobs remain from generation to generation. However, this does not imply that the longstanding values that Gandhi has lived up to and championed will lose their impact. What this implies is that we are going to have to find new and different ways to interpret, recognize, communicate, and live them out. Mahatma Gandhi championed the cause of education and taught students how to be self-reliant and not be subservient to the British. To this cause, he wanted schools to conduct classes in the mother tongue of the region. He was determined that craft education would help students and evoke the correct balance between mechanical and mental labor.

CHAPTER NINE

RABINDRANATH TAGORE'S EDUCATIONAL PHILOSOPHY

Introduction

Rabindranath Tagore was born on 7th May, 1861 in the Jorasanko Mansion in Calcutta. A Bengali polymath, he reshaped his region's literature and music. He became the first non-European to win the Nobel prize for Literature for 'Gitanjali', his book of poems. As a humanist, Universalist, internationalist and strident anti- nationalist he denounced the British Raj and advocated independence from Britain. As an exponent of the Bengal Renaissance, he advanced a vast canon that comprised paintings, sketches and doodles, hundreds of texts, and some two thousand songs; his legacy endures also in the institution he founded, Visva Bharati University. Rabindranath Tagore was a prominent poet and profound thinker. Although he was not educated in any university, he was a clearly a man of learning. He had his own original ideas about education, which led him to establish an educational institution named Vishva Bharati in Shantiniketan with the intention of re-opening the channel of communication between the East and the West. He travelled extensively in different countries of the world, and was a successful mediator between the Eastern and Western cultures.

His short span of school life made him realise that school was a place which tempted to stymie and stifle the native growth of the child and brought untold harm to the development of personality. This heart-felt realisation helped him to formulate his own philosophy of life and of education. At the age of 40, in 1901, he himself established his Shantiniketan Ashram (School) with ten boys only to materialize his own ideas and ideals. This institution turned into a world famous Vishwa Bharati-a seat of international university and a melting point of Eastern and Western culture-a confluence of humanity. An apostle of peace and universal brotherhood he passed away on August 7, 1941 leaving his indelible imprint in the hearts of mankind.

It has been generally accepted that different places have their own culture and tradition. Generally, Western philosophy of education comprises two schools, traditional and modern. It has its roots in Athens, Rome and Judeo-Christianity, whilst Tagore's philosophy of education draws its inspiration from ancient Indian philosophy of education. However, it could be said that Tagore's philosophy of education may become a representation of the Eastern philosophy apart from others like Islam, Confucianism, Taoism, and Mahayana Buddhism. By looking on Western countries and India, both countries have distinct differences in their ways of developing and shaping an individual, in terms of skills and attitudes. Thus, different cultures will have different philosophies, which results in different ways of doing things, especially in educating the next generation.

Western Education in India

Philosophy of education developed by the West was shaped through philosophical thought, which manifested through an idea characterized by Materialism, Idealism, Secularism, and Rationalism. This philosophical thinking, however, affected the concept, interpretation and the definition of the knowledge itself. Rene Descartes, for instance, uses ratio as the sole criteria to measure the truth. Other western philosophers, such as John Locke, Immanuel Kant, Martin Heidegger, Emilio Betti, and Hans-Georg Gadammer, among others, also emphasize the use of ratio and the five senses as their source of knowledge, by which it creates a variety stream of philosophies and thoughts, such as empiricism, humanism, capitalism, existentialism, relativism, atheism, and many others that profoundly affect a number of disciplines, such as philosophy, science, sociology, psychology, politics, economics, and so on.

Consequently, western philosophy of education is not established on revelation or any religious tenets but being established on a cultural tradition strengthened by philosophical speculation bounded by secular life placing man in the centre as a man of ratio. Hence, the science and its ethical and moral values, administered by human ratio always experience changing. According to Syed Naquib Al-Attas, there are five factors underlying western culture and educational philosophies. First, the use of ratio to guide one in his own life, Second, posing duality between reality and truth, Third, emphasizing an existence projecting secular worldview, Fourth, the doctrine of humanism and Fifth, using history as a dominant element in natural tendency and human existence. Those five factors have a very great impact on western intellectual paradigm shaping educational pattern in the west.

British Educational Approach in India

Modern education system in India initially came from British authorities. They initiated Western influence in India. Prior to the advent of the British India, Indian education system was generally private in praxis. In 1835, Lord Macauley introduced modern education in India through Wood's dispatch 1854, generally known as the Magna Charta of Indian education, which becomes the cornerstone of the current Indian education and changed the scenario. By 1857, British power finally consolidated a colonial system of education in India. Its primary aim was to prepare indigenous Indian clerks to handle local administration and the creation of a class of Indians who had been brought up in an English way. In the lower levels of education, the medium of instruction was vernacular languages, whilst for higher education the medium must be in English. British government continuously provided funds to local schools that further made many of them becoming governmentally aided.

Finding it too expensive and impossible practically to import sufficient British to operate and control the rising number of administration branches, British government planned to educate local Indian by the way that they should learn western education and become westernized both culturally and in intellectual achievement. Lord Macauley clearly said that, "we must at present do our best to form a class, who may be interpreters between us and the millions whom we govern; class of persons, Indians in blood and colour, but English in taste, in opinions, in morals and intellect." National universities had been established at Bombay, Madras and Calcutta. The gap between the fortunate upper classes and the vast masses of rural poor continued to widen. A new class of people came to adopt European dress, manners attitudes and life styles. Old values and traditions came to be questioned. And it was a period of social upheaval and reforms in India.

In 1844, Declaration Knowledge of English declared English as a compulsory requirement to apply to government civil services. Due to this condition, Indian traditional education system gradually vanished for the lack of official government support. The government made English medium schools became so much popular that tremendously attracted many Indians. Consequently, traditional occupations also became obsolete.

The British control over education ended with the Indian independence on 15 August 1947. Positively, the British education system created social and political awareness within the country. It inspired literary and cultural consciousness and developed nationalistic awareness. However, it was obviously British-oriented. Its primary aim was to serve British interest and was colonial in aim and practice. The medium of instruction was an obstruction in the development of creativity. Sometimes it encouraged communal passions. The Christian missionaries and the British administrators encouraged Christian teachings within the educational institutions. However, the British philosophy of education in modern period was not conducive to national welfare. It is in this defect of the British philosophy of education as practices in India in modern period that Indian thinkers have bitterly criticized it and one of them was Rabindranath Tagore. Tagore was critical of the British philosophy of education in India. He clearly saw that its aims and means were against Indian interests and thus presented his alternative philosophies, urging Indians to accept steady and purposeful education.

Tagore's Educational Philosophy

Rabindranath Tagore was more than a resounding leading Indian thinker of India in the twentieth century. A prominent figure through his poetic brilliance, Tagore is known to India and the world as the winner of the 1913 Nobel Prize in Literature, the first non-westerner to be honored so. Ramnath Sharma depicted that there are two different thinkers of education in India, the traditional group of Indian philosophers of education on the one hand and the propagators of western philosophy of education on the other, represented by Jawaharlal Nehru and M.N. Roy. While the later were inspired greatly by the Western philosophy of education, the former, including Rabindranath, drew their inspiration from ancient Indian philosophy of education. Drawing their inspiration from ancient Indian philosophy of education, the characteristics of the traditional group can be grouped into four basic aspects: Neo-Vedanta Philosophical Basis, Integral Approach, Integral Psychology, and Synthesis of Idealism and Pragmatism.

He is one among the others, such as Swami Vivekananda, Sri Aurobindo, and Mahatma Gandhi, who bitterly criticized the defects of British philosophy of education. They criticized western educational approach in

India, for its aims and means were against Indian national interest, and thus presented educational philosophies. The questions to which Tagore devotes himself are: What is the aim of education? And how are we to achieve it?

Tagore's Principles of Education

The aim of education, as Rabindranath Tagore sees it, is to give one a sense of one's identity as a total man and to bring education in harmony with life. It is self-realization. He believed that this realization was the goal of education. A total man is the one who thinks of himself first and foremost as human being. What matters to him is not his birth and social status. What crucially matters to him, rather, is the conviction that he is above all a man, irrespective of his socio-economic placing, of his caste, creed, and religion.

The prevalent social condition creates a situation in which the rich family grows up with arrogance and the poor with an inferiority complex. This creates a yawning gap between the two. It is, thus, the process of education that is based on self-realization is extremely needed in order to establish a well-balanced relation with others belonging to different social strata. In order to reach this basic identity of human being, one needs to undertake processes towards this stage of a total man, a process that can only be assisted through education.

Tagore did not find any dichotomy between thought, life and philosophy. Besides, he believed that every human being is one who has potentialities to progress towards the super human being, the universal soul. His conception of the universal soul is derived from the Gita and Upanishadic philosophies. Tagore based his ideas on the ancient Indian thought. Indian tradition believes that man's soul and the universal soul are one, and that self-realization amount to realization of integration with God.

Self-education is based on self-realization, which its process is as important as education itself. The more important thing is that the educator must have faith in himself and universal self, underlying his individual soul. All those actions, which provide a natural sense of contentment, promote educational process. Contentment is a reaction of soul and hence different with merely satisfaction and pleasure. According to Tagore's concept of self-education, the educator has to follow the three following principles:

1. Independence. Tagore believed in a complete freedom of any kind – intellectual freedom, satisfaction, decision, heart, knowledge, actions, and worship. But to achieve this freedom, the student has to practice a calm temperament, harmony, and balance. Through this process the student is able to distinguish between right and wrong, natural and superficial, relevant and irrelevant, permanent and temporal, universal and individual, etc. Consequently, after being able to make this distinction, the student can create a harmony and synthesis in what is right, natural, relevant, permanent, and the real element he has acquired and then turned to self-guidance. This independence is not to be confused with the absence of control, because it is self-control, it implies acting according to one's own rational impulse. Once this level of freedom has been achieved, there is no danger of the individual straying from his path, because his senses, intelligence, emotional feelings and all other powers are directed by his ego.

2. Perfection. Perfection implies that the student must try to develop every aspect of his personality, all the abilities and powers he has been endowed by nature. Therefore, academic learning is not merely to pass examinations, acquiring degrees or certificates with which he fulfils his livelihood. The sole aim of education is development of the child's personality which is possible only when every aspect of the personality is given equal importance, when no part of the personality is neglected and no part is exclusively stressed.

3. Universality. Universality implies the important aspect of an enduring faith in the universal soul, which exists within himself. It is thus important to identify one's own soul with the universal soul. One can search for this universal soul not only within oneself, but in every element of nature and environment. This search is achieved by knowledge, worship and action. Once this realization of the universal soul is achieved, it becomes easier to progress further.

It is, thus, evident from the above principles that the aim of Tagore's pattern of education is independence, perfection, and universality. The educator creates an environment in which the personality of the student undergoes a free, perfect, and unrestricted development.

Tagore's Educational Philosophy vis-à-vis the West

Tagore considered lack of education as the main obstacle in the way of India's progress and at the root of all its problems. Looking upon the western approach on education in India, which emphasized and focused merely on sheer placement in British administration offices and businesses in India, Tagore had bitterly criticized the idea. This had become very important in view of the fact that the civil service was saturated and as the students grew, the majority of graduates failed to get any type of white-collar jobs. The time, however, had come against which Tagore urged to attempt a change in the aims of academic learning and thus offered his own remedial idea.

According to him, academic learning becomes joyless and purely mechanical if it is looked upon merely as an instrument for getting jobs and for material and financial gains. In order to ensure the posit of becoming a total man, the aims of education should be not only as a means to a livelihood, but more importantly to promote awareness of human identity, where one comes into well-balanced relations with others. It means that the end of education is to lead us into how to live meaningfully vis-à-vis the people around us.

However, this does not mean that learning has nothing to do with subsistence, rather it should be aimed at something not only collaborated with pragmatic ends. Academic learning should enable us to understand the situations in which we are placed and to adopt proper attitudes towards them. The attitudes derived from the experiences we have in our lived situations, which involve our relations with the people around us – our relations with families and socio-political surroundings. Because education serves no real purpose in our life if we are unable to connect with the place we are in. As a result, if we are unable to connect with the milieu we are live, thus, it does not stimulate our ideas, nor does it nourish our emotions and imaginations. Tagore criticized the prevalent system of education, which puts too much stress on memory and too little on imagination and thinking.

Tagore highlights the futility of mere scholarship, the idea propounded by some western educational philosophers including Nietzsche. He then criticized any education system whose aim is on the sheer pursuit of knowledge with no end beyond it. Tagore wants to make us aware of the evil of a traditional education system, that is a dry scholarship, which encourages acquisition of static ideas without contributing anything to significant living, an education which remains far away from our life. There must be no gap between ideas or theory and their application to life.

The aim of education should be to develop and nourish our beliefs, emotions, and imaginations, which enable us to assess, evaluate, and take up appropriate attitudes towards our experience in the milieu in which we live. It is this conviction that accounts for Tagore's disapproval of a system of education, which emphasizes too much of theoretical learning. Politics, say, may give us information about the process of democracy, but it cannot become beneficial if it does not bring prosperity to the people.

Tagore viewed the traditional academic learning as merely a knowledge-factory, a mechanical system producing students with machine-ground knowledge for the purpose of being examined and graded. He criticized the idea propounded by Michael Foucault in his *Discipline and Punish* in which he looks at educational institutions on the model of prisons of a disciplinary mechanism involving continuous surveillance, examination, training, punishment. Tagore maintained that the aim of education should not be producing like a machine-made product in a factory, because each individual has a distinctive character of his own. Therefore, education system should attend to it carefully; it should enable each individual to blossom in his own way.

Nature-based Education

Tagore frustrated with the denatured situation of academic learning process and promoted the system on the model of forest solitude or under the open sky. It is by this method that gentle breezes, sunshine, green trees and plants not only to making children physically sound, but to nourishing their minds. He insists that no mind can grow properly without living in intimate communion with nature. Those situations present to the learner a situation, which stimulates his imagination and creativity, and combats the boredom of mechanical learning. In *Tapovan* (The Forest School of India) Tagore asserted that the forest school was typical of the Indian system of education with its emphasis on three basic elements of Indian culture, namely *Advaita* (non-duality) in the field of knowledge, friendship for all in the field offeeling, and fulfilment of one's duties without concern for the outcomes in the field of action.

The ideal school, according to Tagore, should be established away from the turmoil of human habitation under an open sky and surrounded by vistas of fields, trees, and plants. Living in a forest was also associated with austere pursuits and renunciation. The vast background of nature represented a grand perspective against which all objects, all feelings assumed their due proportions. He also referred to the significance of educating feeling as distinct from educating the senses and the intellect. The word 'forest' used in this context, he explained, was not dense jungle, but *Tapovana*, the forest clearing.

Indian national educational system should try to discover the characteristics of the truth of its own civilization. The truth is not commercialism, imperialism or nationalism, but rather universalism. Its aim was to develop individual personality by the means of harmonious interaction and union of the spirit with the environment.

Medium of Education

The medium of education discourse also became an important point pertaining to Tagore's idea. The use of English in education prevented assimilation of what was taught and made education confined only to urban areas and the upper classes rather than rural areas. Therefore, if the vast rural masses were to benefit, it was absolutely essential to switch over to the use of Bengali in the context of Bengal at all level of education. Tagore believed that without knowledge pattern of rural living and an effort by the school to revitalize rural life, academic learning would be incomplete. And this is the reason behind the establishment of his own university, popularly known as Visva Bharati.

Tagore stressed on the unnaturalness of the system of education in India, its lacks of links with the nation and its management, which was in the hands of a foreign government. The working of the government, its court of law and its education system were conducted in a language completely meaningless to the majority of Indians. He contrasted the situation in India with what he had seen in the USSR and in Japan, where the governments had been able to educate their people within a very short time. He argued that to educate India's entire population and restoring the flow of culture from the educated classes to the rural population would not come about unless the mother-tongue was adopted as the medium of teaching.

Education as a Means of Peace

Another point from the British education result that Tagore had also criticized was the fact that the British educational process failed to develop attitudes and the spirit of inquiry. Moreover, it divided Indian people into two classes: those who received British education and those who did not. The former, comprising everyone taking from the wealthy, educated and English speaking class living in cities and towns, whilst the latter remained almost everyone living in the countryside.

Tagore wanted science to be taught along with India's own philosophical and spiritual knowledge at Indian universities. Because science without constraint of self-knowledge leads to an endless desire for material goods and well-being, and the meaningless pursuit of the instruments of war and power, which are often the origin of conflict among nations and the source of suppression of the weaker by the stronger. That is why both spiritual and scientific knowledge are considered by Tagore as equally important. About the place of religion in education, Tagore said: "Nature and human spirit wedded together would constitute our temple and selfless good deeds our worship."

R.N Tagore's Philosophy:

His philosophy is an amalgamation of humanism, individualism, naturalism, idealism, realism, spiritualism, internationalism and nationalism. Tagore remarked, **"I have great faith in humanity like the sun it can be clouded, but never extinguished."**

On Tagore's of life there is a powerful impression and influence of religious, highly cultured and philosophy loving family to which he belonged. He imbibed the Idealistic philosophy of life and adopted the highest ideals of Truth, Beauty and Goodness as the chief aims of education to be achieved by all human beings. As an Idealist, Tagore believed in the absolute and immortal existence of God, but he believed in God as a Superman of 'Monism'. As such, he writes-**"We should try to search for God and thus realize that truth which will liberate us from material bonds of existence and which is capable to illuminate the whole world with its divine light."**

Tagore's Philosophy of Education:

Tagore has emphasized that among human beings, nature and international relations there exists a basic unity and love. Hence, true education should promote this fellow-feeling and love in all the present things. Education prevalent in the days of Tagore was right, logical and so lifeless that it did not confirm to needs of individual and demand of Society.

Tagore's philosophy of education conforms to his general philosophy. Factors which influenced Tagore's educational philosophy were influence of home environment, love for nature, love for nation, his extensive visits abroad and influence of school environment.

The origin of Tagore's educational theory was his own home life and the freedom he had experienced with it. Education prevalent in the days of Tagore was rigid and lifeless.

Hence, he deadly opposed the current education and insisted that education should acquaint the child with the voice and mission of individual as well as international life and achieve a harmonious balance between all the factors being free from all compulsions and restrictions.

Tagore recommended that education should be provided in the company of Nature which will strengthen the ties between man and Nature. Both man and Nature are the creations of one and the same God. He considered Nature as a powerful agency for the moral and spiritual development of the child exerting a very healthy influence upon the heart, mind and body of the child. Under the natural and healthy environment, pupils can find a natural outlet for their capacities and great chance of their development. He was of the firm view that education is a vehicle of social reform. Hence, it should act as a life-giving current to modern society serving in various ways. He advocated that education should be according to the realities of life. Any education cut away from life is useless. Hence, any plan of education should involve both nature and needs of man in a harmonious programme.

Believing in harmonious relationships of man with man, with surroundings and international relations, Tagore advocated that a man through the process of education should be able to come out as a harmonious individual in tune with his social set of life. The highest education is that which does not merely give us information but makes our life in harmony with all existence.

Tagore was not in favour of mere intellectual development. He stressed that education should promote creative self-expression. He suggested that creative self-expression can be promoted through subjects of life crafts, music, drawing and dramatics. The environment of freedom given to the learner and then creating situations for him will automatically make the learner to do something original.

Teacher: Tagore gave a very important place to the teacher. He assigned an important role to him in the education of child believing that only man can teach another man. To him, the teacher is a Guru like ancient Indian Rishis who is to keep the students on the right track by remaining a learner throughout his life. A teacher is to stimulate and guide but it is the child who is to choose and react according to his natural inclinations. Believing in purity and innocence of child, the teacher should behave with him with great love, affection, sympathy and consideration. Tagore also stated that the teachers and students are considered to be learners together, seeking truth and following the right path of pure simplicity as well as renunciation. The teacher should always be busy with motivating the creative capacities of children so that they remain busy with constructive activities and experiences.

Classroom Teaching: Tagore did not approve the traditional methods of class-room teaching. He recommended those methods which provide knowledge of concrete situations. He favoured frequent excursions and tours, during which the pupils with their senses alert might observe and learn various facts of interest. Education must be given in geographical, historical, economic and cultural perspectives. In order to enable children to learn new things, it is necessary to maintain an educative atmosphere where children are not compelled to learn things from text-books, but from the natural surroundings which are most educative.

'Shanti Nikaten experiment:

Tagore was a great philosopher and educationist. He expressed himself in these capacities by his own efforts. He was born in a family which was well known for its progressive views, social and cultural attainments, political awakening and also a centre for the struggle of independence. Artists, poets, dramatists, musicians, scientists and philosopher belonged to this family. Tagore's grasping imbibing powers were so acute and sensitive that he inculcated all the refinements in his family. This self –education developed Tagore's inherent capacities of the fullest extent.

At Shantiniketan, under the environment of the ashram; the pupils find the best opportunity for their physical, intellectual and spiritual development. Being members of their school community, they learn their lesson of citizenship in a large society and the activities of the school are planned and organized by the teachers to closely connect pupils with society by having opportunities of drawing inspiration directly from their own folk literature, traditions and also receiving instructions through the medium of their own.

1. Teachers should create good human relationships in society.

2. Teachers should have knowledge of economic and social problems of society.

3. Teachers should co-operate community to solve various problems.

4. Teachers should be dedicated to the welfare of society.

5. Teachers should work for community sanitation.

6. Teachers should respect ancient Indian culture.

7. Teachers should provide adult education to society.

Shantiniketan brought Tagore a spark of immortality. Popularly it means an abode of peace took its shape in 1901 and turned into an international university, named VishwaBharati in 1921. VishwaBharati became a National University in 1951.

Situated at Bolpur, 100 miles away from Calcutta Shantiniketan Ashram had beautiful surroundings. Life at Shantiniketan was very simple and it was a residential institution having self-governing Republic. Pupils were taught the art of managing their own affairs smoothly.

There was perfect community life at Shantiniketan, with common dining, cooperative living, and freedom was the watchword of the institution. Love, sympathy, joy and peace scented the institution. Full-scale opportunities were given to pupils for realizing their potentialities. It was a community school without any distinction on the basis of caste, creed and other forms of distinction.

This school became an international university in 1921 with the following purposes:

The institution has to teach the culture of the East. A synthesis of eastern culture and that of western culture is to be made possible for facilitating unification of mankind. The institution has to prepare itself for the work of the rural reconstruction with a view to ameliorating the condition of poor and deprived people.

There prevailed a serene atmosphere amidst joy and freedom and nobility and co-operation. The work of the institution starts from 5 O'clock in the early morning and it continues till afternoons emphasizing subjects and activities. Perfect discipline overshadows the institution. There is perfect inter-personal relationship in the institution. Students from far and near, east and west are enrolled into it.

There is complete fusion of occidental and oriental culture with a view to fostering international understanding. It stands as a cosmopolitan university. The motto of ViswaBharati is, "Where the whole world forms its one single unit." It is regarded as modern Nalanda without barriers. It belongs to the humanity as a whole. There have different sections and departments in it, viz. Sishu Bhawan, Path Bhawan, Kala Bhawan, Sangit Bhawan, Sriniketan (Department of Rural Reconstruction) Silpa Sadan, Cheen Bhawan, Rabindra Bhawan, Hindi Bhawan, the institute for studies in Islamic culture, etc.

In short, Viswabharati University is the unique contribution of Gurudev Tagore where four-fold principles of education are followed, viz, freedom, creative self-expression, active communion with the nature and man and internationalism. It preaches spiritual unity of mankind and universal brotherhood. Rural development through education is another chief contribution of Tagore. His concept of freedom and teacher still brings him immortality which the present generation and posterity cannot forget. He, unlike Rousseau, was a realist giving practical shape to his ideology. He made a happy blend between the two opposite cultures-western and eastern through his brain-child-Viswabharati. Moreover, his thrust upon creativity by means of an array of activities is truly laudable and recognised by the humanity. In fact, he is a humanist.

Concept of Education: Tagore was deadly against the then prevalent system of education which snatched the child from the laps of Nature very early in life, confined him within the boundaries of school and then put him into an office or factory.

Educational Aims as propounded by Rabindranath Tagore:

1. Education should aim to develop the child physically. Tagore believed that a healthy mind lives in a healthy body.

2. Education should enable the child to acquire the knowledge through independent efforts and critical examination of ideas.

3. Education should inculcate moral and spiritual values in children.

4. Chief aim of education should be drawing out all the latent potentialities of child.

5. Education should create self-discipline among teachers as well as children.

6. Education should aim at the attainment of inner freedom, inner power and enlightenment.

7. Education should not only train children to be effective farmers, clerks or craftsmen, but also develop them to be complete human beings.

8. Education should aim at development of a sense of social service in pupils and teachers.

Tagore in 'The Religion of Man' (1931) while describing true position of a teacher among students states that a teacher is the infinite ideal of man towards whom the students move in their collective growth. They find their ideal of father, friend and beloved among teachers.

Going further in the same source, Tagore has a clear knowledge about the educational implications of adolescents and in his schools, he adopts necessary principles and special measures to keep off the problems arising out of the emotional maladjustment of the adolescents. In the transition period, the students become very much sensitive and tender dealings make them happy. In such period,

1. Teachers should be dedicated to their profession.

2. Teachers should be embodiment of moral, mental and spiritual values.

3. Teachers should always remain learners.

4. Teachers should have feeling of brotherhood and fatherhood.

The pupils sometimes become tumultuous but where the teacher-taught relationship is natural and sweet, these disturbances are swept away like refuges in flood water.

Highlighting the idea of partnership between teachers and taught, Tagore, stands stated that education is a joint venture of both the teacher and the pupil. He adds to his statement believing that the pupils share the experiences of life with his teacher but it is the teacher who selects the desirable experiences to expose before the pupils and to guard them against the undesirable ones.

Tagore considers teachers to be of paramount importance in any scheme of education. He desires teachers to help young children to grow on their own as a gardener helps the young plants to grow. Tagore wants his students to acquire a scientific temper, to stimulate constructive doubt, the love of mental adventure, the courage and longing to conquer the world by enterprise and boldness in thought and in action.

Aims of Education:R. N. Tagore has not written any book on education, yet from his writings and speeches, one can find out that the aims of education which he prescribed were almost the same as were advocated by our ancient seers and saints. In the following lines, we discuss the chief aims of education as advocated by Tagore:

Physical Development: R. N. Tagore believed that a healthy mind lives in a healthy body.Tagore emphasized the physical well-being of the children. In order to achieve this, he said that education in nature; play activities, dancing, exercise, body and sensory training were the tools. Education of the body is necessary for acquiring the capacity to adjust itself to all sorts of weather conditions and health hazards.

Moral and Spiritual Aims: Tagore said that the principal aim of education should be the development of moral and spiritual aspects of the child's personality. For this, he emphasized upon inner development, attainment of inner freedom, inner power and enlightenment. One of the important objectives of starting Shantiniketan was 'to give spiritual culture to our boys." Education should enable the child to realize self and help them to develop the self-force. He wanted to develop an unflinching faith in the spiritual force. Further, he stressed moral training and development of character through austere devotion and development of inner discipline.

Intellectual Development: Condemning the prevailing system of education as bookish, methodical, monotonous, examination-oriented, where intellect was starved of intellectual nourishment and where we adorned the cage but the parrot within lays starving. Tagore wanted education should aim at cultivating the power of acquiring ideas through independent effort, curiosity and alertness of mind, and the potentiality of critically appraising the ideas, of assimilating them and of using what we learn. Education should develop thinking and imagination rather than mere memory or storage of scattered information.

Education for Fullness: According to Tagore, the aim of education should be harmonious development of all human faculties. In other words, education should aim at making a man full or complete without neglecting one at the cost of other.

Cardinal Principles of Tagore's Educational Philosophy: Tagore was influenced by the book 'Robinson Crusoe'. According to him man and nature have an original integration. The three cardinal principles of Tagore's educational philosophy are **(1) Freedom; (2) Active communication with Nature and man; (3) Creative self-expression.** Tagore felt that education divorced from the streams of life and confined within four walls becomes artificial and loses its value. Tagore believed in self-imposed discipline which is not imposed from outside but drawn out from within.

Tagore's Curriculum: Tagore was dead against the prevailing British system of education which was life-less, monotonous, listless, useless, colourless, lop-sided, purely academic, and dissociated from the life-line of the society. In his scheme of education he has struck a balance between the education of the nature and education of man, and between the culture of east and the that of west (oriental and occidental culture), His curriculum was flexible, dynamic and child-centred and aimed at development of personality in all its aspects.

He emphasized a list of subjects, albeit, he did not favour book learning and he wanted the best book was the 'Nature' where the child would get adequate knowledge. He favoured the study of mother-tongue and at the higher level of education; he favoured learning of English to know the treasure of knowledge in the fields of culture, literature and science. He also suggested the study of world history, culture of India, literature, geography, science etc. Besides he suggested the following activities for the promotion of aesthetic and emotional faculties. They are music, fine arts, painting, drawing, dance, dramatics, and crafts like book-binding, carpentry, weaving, serving, gardening etc. Moreover, Tagore stressed upon community living and community services for the realization of truth from the standpoint of spiritual development. To sum up, his curricular framework emphasized subjects, activities and services.

Tagore's Methods of Teaching: He believed in activity and dynamic methods of teaching based upon the interest, need, experience, attitude, ability and mental development of the child. He labelled the then system of teaching as bookish, mechanical, stereotyped, dull and uninteresting. Therefore, he strongly suggested independent study and efforts (heuristic method). Learning should proceed from familiar to unfamiliar, near to far and known to unknown. Learning should be linked with joy and ecstasy. He wanted to give education in a natural surroundings characterised by freedom and creativity. He said that teaching while walking is the best method of teaching. He suggested that social science subject could be better taught through excursions and study tours. He favoured discussion and activity or learning by doing method. Tagore considered the following methods of teaching as proper and effective-

1.   Teaching While Walking
2.   Discussion and Question- Answer Method
3.   Activity Method.

Conclusion

Rabindranath Tagore, by his efforts and achievements, is one of a global network of pioneering educators, who have striven to create non-authoritarian learning systems appropriate to their respective surroundings. Tagore did not neglect the lesser aim of life and education, where the focus of colonial system of education was ultimately on employment. His intention was to correct this conception, without ignoring science, technology, and efforts on rural empowerment. For without these, it is impossible to revive the poor condition of people living in rural areas.

Tagore felt that young generation should aware of their national cultural heritage, grasp its significance for them, and persuaded them to learn cultures from other countries. Tagore put great emphasis on the use of a national language as the vehicle of education at all stages of education. He wanted Indian universities to integrate themselves with society and make an effort to educate people living in the countryside. Conclusively, he did not want education to remain confined to the cities and to particular classes of society.

CHAPTER TEN

EDUCATIONAL PHILOSOPHY OF SWAMI VIVEKANANDA

Introduction

"Talk to yourself once in a day, otherwise you may miss meeting an intelligent person in this world". -Swami Vivekananda.

Swami Vivekananda was born on 12th January 1863. Swamiji's original name was Narendranath Datta. He acquired the new name in 1886 when he took 'Sanyasa'. Under the influence of his mother, he made a deep study of Hindu scriptures. Vivekananda had an excellent command over Bengali, English and Sanskrit. He was equally adaptable in boxing, riding, swimming, and wrestling. He was an ardent student of philosophy and poetry. His Principle Rev. W. W. Hastic complimenting Vivekananda once remarked, "Narendranath is really a genius. I have never yet come across a lad of his talents and possibilities, even in German universities, among philosophical students." A turning point in his life took place when he met Ramakrishna Paramhansa, at Dakhineswar in 1882. This meeting with his Guru brought a spiritual transformation within him. His knowledge of India left him deeply affected by the despair and poverty of the masses of India. On September 11, 1893, Swamiji made a soul-stirring address at the World Parliament of Religions at Chicago (USA). In his address, he said that upon the banner of every religion will soon be written, "Help and not Fight", "Assimilation and not Destruction", "Harmony and Peace and not Dissension". Swamiji devoted the rest of his life to communicating the message of unity, tolerance, sacrifice and brotherhood. He breathed his last in the year 1902 with the assertion that Indians can be happy and free only by the application of Vedanta in their lives. He popularized that India should practice strength-giving religion and a man-making education.

Swami Vivekananda's Philosophy of life:

ax. The Draita, the Visita-draita and the Advaita are the various expressions of the Vedanta. And Swamiji was a true Vedantist. Swamiji asserted that the various expression of Vedanta are the stages for helping the individual to proceed progressively towards the realization of higher ideals and thus leading everything to get merged in the wonderful unity with the creator.

ax. According to Swamiji God exists in three forms- (i) He is infinite existence. (ii) He is infinite knowledge. (iii) He is infinite bliss. And as God resides in every human heart, so all these three attributes of God exist in the human heart.

ax. Swamiji said, "The only God to worship is the human soul, in the human body". In fact, he found the manifestation of God in man.

ax. Swamiji believed in every religion. He regarded every religion to be equal. All religions lead to the same goal, that is for the good of mankind.

ax. Swami Vivekananda believed in universalism and spiritual brotherhood.

ax. According to Swami Vivekananda, "Perfection is not to be attained, it is already within us. Immortality and bliss are not to be acquired, we already have that".

Swami Vivekananda's Philosophy of Education:

The main elements of the philosophy of Swami Vivekananda are as follows:-

ax. The human mind is the storehouse of all knowledge.

ax. No knowledge comes from outside. It is inherent in man.

ax. Man discovers the knowledge that is in his mind.

ax. Education is the manifestation of the perfection already in man.

ax. Mind is the owner of the infinite library of the universe.

Basic Principles of Educational Philosophy of Vivekananda:

ax. The human mind is the mother of all knowledge. No knowledge is external. Every knowledge is built internally. The external world provides only the platform or the occasion to study one's mind and process the ultimate knowledge.

ax. Vivekananda believed in self-education. He asserts that a child learns by himself. The teacher provides the environment for the child for his growth.

ax. Every soul is the soul of God – says Swamiji. So, every child is a God. The purpose of adult including the teacher is to serve the child according to his needs.

ax. Swami Vivekananda believed in universal education. He advocated that education is the birthright of every child and it is only education that can eradicate the poverty of the masses.

ax. He strongly believed that concentration is at the root of all education and brings success in life.

ax. Vivekananda advocated Brahmacharya. According to him, Brahmacharya gives mental and spiritual power of the highest kind.

ax. Vivekananda raised a voice for women education for their character formation and self-identity.

ax. He believed in the realization of religion. One must experience true religion from within.

ax. Swami Vivekananda believed in the national system of education which includes the mind to know about Indian culture, philosophy and civilization.

ax. He believed in the symphony of eastern philosophy and western science.

ax. Education for the masses was his slogan. He said that "The great national sin is the neglect of the masses and that is one of the chief causes of our downfall. No amount of politics would be of any avails until the masses, in India are once more well educated, well-fed and created for. We must work for them".

Swami Vivekananda on Various Aspects of Education:

According to Swamiji, "Education is the manifestation of the perfection already present in man". He believed that education is not simply giving or storing information. He said, "If educational were identicalwith information, the libraries would be the greatest sages in the world and encyclopedias the Rishis". He believed in man's education to win in the struggle for life. Therefore the concept of education in his own words reads, "We want that education by which character has formed the strength of mind is increased, the intellect is expanded and by which one stands on one's own feet.

Aims of education:

ax. Development of character by practising Brahmacharya, which helps in the development of mental, moral, and spiritual powers for contributing good to others and developing courage, fearlessness and strength for a noble cause.

ax. Moral and spiritual development to create a human being and a spirit of fellow-being.

ax. As knowledge is inherent in man, the aim of education is to discover the knowledge that lies hidden in our mind and thus helping for mental development.

ax. Swamiji believed that physical development and education can help in the growth of elf-realisation and character building.

ax. Every education should lead an individual to stand on his own feet. Or otherwise, it is useless. To achieving vocational efficiency, Vivekananda recommended training in agriculture and industry.

ax. According to Swami Vivekananda, one of the essential aims of education is religious development which helps to find the absolute truth or reality.

ax. Education must teach man that soul is the same in all and thus promote universal brotherhood.

ax. Education should help to develop faith in oneself. The aim of developing faith is one's own self, shraddha and the spirit of renunciation is a must.

ax. The true aim of education is to develop in oneself the feeling of unity in diversity.

Curriculum:

ax. Swami Vivekananda believed in fostering material welfare with spiritual development. He advocated the inclusion of all such subjects in the curriculum that lead to the development of materialistic and spiritual identities. On one hand, he stressed the study of Vedanta, Upanishads, Puranas, Religion and Philosophy for spiritual development while on the other, he stated the importance of scientific education.

ax. Vivekananda believed that as science is the mechanism behind the existence of life, so, art supplies meaning to that existence and thus art is inseparable from life. Hence education in science must be supplemented by the teaching of arts.

ax. Vivekananda advocated that the practice of a common language will unify the country more strongly.

ax. He felt the need to encourage every regional language because it is the mother tongue of the child.

ax. Vivekananda strongly believed that Sanskrit is the source of all Indian languages. He advocated that the knowledge of Sanskrit bring awareness in us regarding our cultural heritage and past greatness. The study of Sanskrit brings stability and permanence to the progress of our country.

ax. Vivekananda also supported the inclusion of subjects like History, Geography, Economics, Mathematics, Home Science, Psychology and Agriculture.

ax. He felt the need for physical education both for self-realisation and character building.

Methods of teaching-learning:

ax. Vivekananda advocated in self-teaching – "No one was ever taught by another. Each of us has to teach himself. A child educates itself".

ax. The teacher is a living example that was believed by Vivekananda. "Words even thoughts, contribute only one-third of the influence in making an impression and the man two-third".

ax. True teaching lies in positive thoughts. The use of kind words provides encouragement and subsequent improvement.

ax. The power of concentration is the way to the storehouse of knowledge. And so, Vivekananda promoted the practice of Brahmacharya.

ax. He asserted that the students can be kept on their right way through the method of guidance and counselling.

ax. Vivekananda was an ardent supporter of freedom in education. He believed the true education cannot be achieved under external discipline. Education is only possible only through free discipline.

ax. Vivekananda advocated discussion and contemplation be followed in education. The student can remove the difficulties in his way of discussing them with his teacher in a formal and informal atmosphere.

ax. To develop divine wisdom, Vivekananda encouraged the utilization of imitation quality of children.

ax. He advocated activity learning. Learning through activities mean it can provide direct experience to the children. He also advocated for the introduction of activities like excursion, camp etc; to help the students to understand the value of social service.

Role of a teacher:

ax. The attitude of a teacher in the teaching-learning process should be like a worshipper.
ax. A teacher should provide a healthy environment to his students.
ax. The nature of a teacher should be like a friend, philosopher and guide and thus helping to go forward in his own way.
ax. A teacher should have knowledge of scriptures.
ax. A teacher should be a role model of high character.
ax. He should culture love and humanity among his students.

Place of a child in education: Vivekananda stated, "Go into your own and get the Upanishads out of your own self. You are the greatest book that ever was or will be. Until the inner teacher opens, all outside teaching is in vain". Swamiji advocated for child-centric education. Swamiji believed that knowledge resides within every child and the teacher should allow the child to grow naturally and spontaneously.

Discipline: Swamiji believed in free discipline. He asserted that every child should be allowed to discipline himself by his own power. There is no discipline in existence when exerted from outside.

Conclusion

Swami Vivekananda was a great educationist who dreamed of a modern India enriched with ancient wisdom. Swamiji's knowledge of Vedanta led him to believe in the advocation of self-knowledge, self-reliance, courage, faith, concentration, Brahmacharya, women education and education for the masses. Vivekananda asserted that real education leads to the development of brotherhood of man, the realization of God, renunciation and righteousness. Swamiji's views on education can be summed up by saying that what he advocated years ago bears relevance to education in present India with perennial applicability. His message was not limited to a nation, it extended its wings to the quality development of the whole humanity of the world.

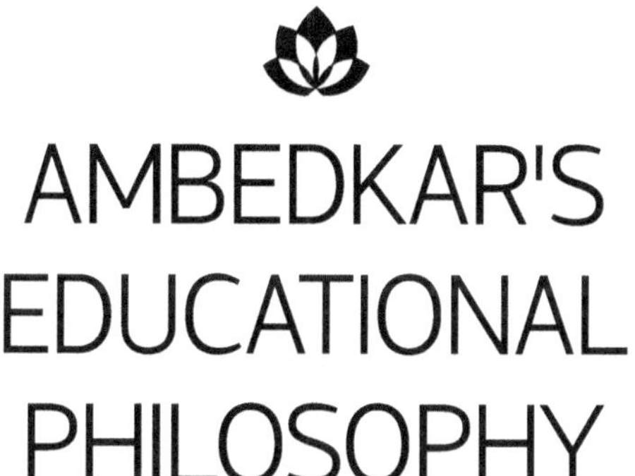

CHAPTER ELEVEN

AMBEDKAR'S EDUCATIONAL PHILOSOPHY

Introduction

"The education that makes us neither competent nor teaches us lessons of equality and morality is no more education." – Dr.Bhimrao Ramji Ambedkar

Education is important for social advancement. It aids man in overcoming the stifling effects of prejudice and superstition, allowing him to realise his full potential. It makes man aware of his rights and responsibilities to his fellow beings. As a result, education is the most effective way of achieving an inclusive society and a critical tool for social progress. Dr. B. R. Ambedkar was a world-renowned philosopher, orator, erudite academic, and prolific journalist. Education, economics, sociology, law, democracy, anthropology, political science, theology, and philosophy are among the topics included in his writings. Dr. Ambedkar ushered in a new era of social awakening, as well as a sense of social importance and self-assurance among the underprivileged. He fought the Hindu social order relentlessly for social inclusion, individual dignity, and political and economic emancipation. His main goal was to raise social and political awareness among India's Dalits about their human rights. He encouraged them to use schooling, organisation, and agitation to plan for a revolution. According to Dr. Ambedkar, philosophy's true purpose is not only to justify the essence of the universe, but also to encourage man to change it in order to make it a better place to live. Despite the fact that philosophy encompasses a wide variety of topics, Dr. Ambedkar approached philosophy in his own unique manner. Philosophy has a social and ethical sense for Dr. Ambedkar because he intended it to be a tool for social reform. In a more profound sense, Ambedkar was a social scientist. "Philosophy has its origins in life's challenges, and any ideas philosophy proposes must return to civilization as tools of societal reconstruction," he says. Knowing is insufficient. All who know must strive to achieve." Dr. Ambedkar sought to use education as an instrument to transform society by applying his social theory to it. He emphasises the importance of educating the poor for the society's true social and economic growth. In this article, an effort is made to evaluate Dr. Ambedkar's views on education and to investigate his educational theory. It would also attempt to comprehend Dr. B. R. Ambedkar's educational theory in the twenty-first century.

Dr. Ambedkar, a great thinker and his contribution to Education

Dr. Ambedkar was dissatisfied with the schooling system in place at the time. He advocated for mass education since the education system at the time excluded the lower classes (shudras/dalits) and women. There was no dignity or educational rights. Dalits were mentally slaves, intellectually degraded, spiritually handicapped, economically frail, and socially backward as a result of their lack of schooling, and they lacked social rank and honour. Ambedkar's guru, Mahatma Jotirao Phule, put in a lot of effort, and for the first time in India, schools for the education of women and untouchables were built. . It was Ambedkar who first proposed the concept of free and compulsory education in order for impoverished people, known as dalits, to get an education because they lacked the financial means to pay for it. He prescribed several provisions concerning education in the constitution, including Articles 28, 29, 30, 45, 46, and 350.

Meaning of Education

Education is important for social advancement. It aids man in overcoming the stifling effects of prejudice and superstition, allowing him to realise his full potential. It makes man aware of his rights and responsibilities to his fellow beings. As a result, education is the most effective way of achieving an inclusive society and a critical tool for social progress. "Education is not only a human being's birthright, but also a tool of social change," said Dr. Bhimrao Ramji Ambedkar.

Education of the downtrodden, the Dalits, is essential for the society's true social and economic growth. For him, schooling is more than just a way of preparing for a career; it is a strong tool that liberates people from ignorance and gives them the courage to combat inequality and shame.

"Education is what makes a person fearless, what gives him the lesson," Dr. Ambedkar said. It instils in him a sense of belonging, makes him mindful of his interests, and motivates him to fight for them." "Educate, Unite, Agitate," he said.

Aims of Education

Dr. Ambedkar was a Buddhist philosopher who called for the cultivation of virtue in humans. He stressed goals that are important and contribute to the happiness and prosperity of humanity as well as the advancement of society. Many evils pervaded at the time of Dr. Ambedkar, one of which being untouchability. Dr. Ambedkar discovered that the people of India are mental slaves and trained, so he put a strong emphasis on mental growth, scientific mentality, and vocational development.

Social emancipation: Education's primary goal is to change individuals' social, fiscal, and political circumstances. Dr. Ambedkar was an outspoken critic of casteism, untouchability, racial injustice, social inequalities, women's inequality, and other forms of oppression. Education, he believed, was critical in eliminating current social inequalities and oppression in Indian society and establishing dignity, brotherhood, coexistence, and mutual acceptance. 'Education is not only a human being's birth right, but also a tool of social transformation,' he claimed.

Universalization of education: Dr. Ambedkar was a staunch follower of his friend John Dewey's vision of educational democratisation. Owing to India's prevailing socioeconomic injustice, a significant portion of the population has been denied access to education for a long time. Dr. Ambedkar believed that education is a natural right that everyone has and that no one can be refused it. As a result, a democratic country should provide equal access to education to all members of its population.

Women Education: "I assess the success of the society by the degree of progress which women have achieved," he said in a lecture on the 20th of July 1942 in Nagpur. He was adamant that if half of the country's population remained uneducated, India, like no other country on the planet, would be unable to advance. Dr. Ambedkar was a keen advocate of women's education as a real nationalist and social reformer. He was well aware that women's education is critical for the advancement of society and the growth of the region. 'Education is as important for women as it is for men,' he said. There will be a lot of improvement if you could read and write.'

Women's role in social empowerment through education: Dr. Ambedkar believed that educated women could make a significant contribution to social progress. She is the family's closest relative and the child's first teacher since she is a mum. They should instil in their children good qualities and virtues. As a result, he encouraged women to pursue higher education. 'I'll tell you a few things that I think you should keep in mind,' he said. Learn to maintain a tidy house and abstain from all vices. Give your children an education. Instill a sense of ambition in them. Instill in them the belief that they are destined for greatness. Remove all inferiority complexes from them.

Focus on religious education and character development: Dr. Ambedkar believed that education without moral ideals should not really be considered education. He was a true believer that if moral ideals and character development are not prioritised in education, a well-educated individual would be of little benefit to society. He said, "An learned man lacking character and modesty is more deadly than a beast," in a speech to the Bombay province Depressed Classes Youth Conference on February 12, 1938. The learned man is a curse to humanity if his education is harmful to the health of the poor... Education is less necessary than character.'

Many historians agree that Dr. Ambedkar not only opposed faith and culture in school, but that he also accepted Karl Marx's famous quote about religion being "the people's opium." In reality, he saw religion and culture as necessary components of education. However, there is no denying that he was opposed to social disparities and religious practices. He emphasised the value of faith, saying, "Whatever positive qualities I have in me or whatever advantages my education has brought to society, I owe them to the religious feelings in me." He added, "I want religion, but I don't want irony in religion."

Job-oriented and skill-based schooling: One of the main goals of education is to prepare people to work for a living or to become self-sufficient. Dr. Ambedkar recognised the importance of work or making a living in one's life. He felt that schooling would only be deemed complete until an ability was combined with it, and that skill would result in the individual being able to find work. As a result, he placed a strong emphasis on vocational education, which he saw as essential for the advancement of society's poor and backward classes.

The importance of mother-tongue and foreign languages in education: Language is the most important instrument for learning. The basic theory of education is that if education is delivered in the child's mother tongue, the child can understand it more easily. Dr. Ambedkar called for mother tongue education while also requiring each pupil to know at least one foreign language. So that he will keep up with global developments in his field and consider what is going on around the globe. Furthermore, many people are unaware that during the Constituent Assembly conference, Dr. Ambedkar suggested making Sanskrit the national or state language.

Role of Teacher: Dr. Ambedkar believed that a teacher was critical to a student's overall progress. He was of the opinion that if we have good teachers, we would be able to produce good pupils. Teachers were held in high esteem by him, and he was helped in granting them a prominent position. He believed that the most significant factor in the growth of a stable and full human identity is the instructor. A effective teacher should approach all members of society with a constructive and egalitarian perspective. He advocated for teachers' credentials and other skills to be scrutinised only when they are hired in schools or college.

Role of Students: Dr. Ambedkar expects students to be unwavering and admirable in their pursuit of knowledge. Students should be eager to learn at all times. And, the student should be mindful of and concerned about his fitness. Educational institutions, according to Ambedkar, should be an assembly of the educated, a body of thinkers who have been fighting for the advancement of wisdom, its proliferation and transmission, and through which they have been trying to form men. It should have a safe atmosphere, and every child, regardless of class, caste, or gender, should be able to receive an education there. Ambedkar found primary school to be the most important of the schools because the aura of the school makes an indelible imprint on a child's soft mind when he leaves the courtyard of his parents' home. As it was clear that education for all classes was difficult to come by at the time, he founded educational institutions in various parts of Maharashtra. He founded colleges and provided opportunities for Dalits to pursue higher education, which are now known as Siddhartha Mahavidyalaya and Milind Mahavidyalaya.

Conclusion: To summarise, Dr. Ambedkar's educational theory is a synthesis of ancient and contemporary education. Dr. Ambedkar's work is important because he emphasised the need for educational advancement for a wide segment of Indian society that has been deprived of education for a long time. Dr. Ambedkar was a key figure in the formulation of several legislation relating to education and social emancipation for oppressed people during the formation of the Indian constitution. It's important to recognise that if a significant portion of population has access to education, society will never be able to progress holistically. It is important to bridge the social divide; otherwise, social stability would be impossible to achieve. As a result, Dr. Ambedkar emphasised that the state should provide universal quality education as well as technical education to the people so that social and economic equity can be developed in our society and our country can advance.

CHAPTER TWELVE

CONTRIBUTIONS OF RAJA RAM MOHAN ROY

Introduction

Nearly 200 years ago, when evils like -- Sati -- plagued the society, when superstations and darkness of fake prejudices captured our society, when British Government conspired to destroy the brotherhood among the Indians through religion, when education system of Indian faces a detrimental phase, the man who played a critical role to bring about a change not only in the religious views of the people but also the social and progressive educational changes is Raja Ram Mohan Roy. He opposed the regressive practice that forced a widow to immolate herself on husband's pyre. He advocated the right of women to be remarried and educated themselves. That time he was the only one who challenged traditional Hindu culture and indicated lines of progress for Indian society under British rule and called the father of modern India.

Raja Ram Mohan Roy was a great scholar and independent thinker and a multilingual person. He believed that education was the only key for progression of Indian society. He introduced Western learning into Indian education system. For that he promoted study of English, Science, Western Medicine and Technology in India. IN Bengal Renaissance, Raja Ram Mohan Roy is regarded as one of the most important figure.

Here in this article we will discuss about the contributions and the ideology of Raja Ram Mohan Roy. We also highlight the similarities among his ideologies and Modern Educational pattern also.

Contributions of Raja Ram Mohan Roy:

Synthesizer of Eastern and Western Education: The union between the western and eastern culture was the great contribution of Raja Ram Mohan Roy as an educationist. He was one of the earliest Indians to realize that

India's greatest need was a composite version of Eastern and Western cultures. At the same time, he understood that only Western Literature and Science can complete the missing essential qualities which eastern education lacks. He believed that if these disciplines were good for British, then they are good for Indians too. Despite many criticism and allegations of being unpatriotic, he was responsible for the paradigm shift of cultural and educational reforms in India through his ideas. He believed that it was better for Indians to take the good things from west and infuse it with traditional knowledge to produce unique results.

English, a part of Indian Education system: Besides realizing the value of Western Science and thought, he always supported English education. He believed that it could generate a sense of unity among the Indian educated youths. His ideas of western education helped the Government of Lord William Bentinck to introduce European learning in India.

Contribution in the field of Language: Ram Mohan Roy's great contribution to the system of modern education and modern Indian languages were highly valuable for the society. He himself gave a great lead in the matter by writing books in Bengali on Grammar, Geography, Astronomy and Geometry and he is considered as the father of modern literary Bengali prose. Raja Ram Mohan Roy also studied Persian and Arabic along with Sanskrit, which influenced his thinking about God. He read Upanishads, Vedas and the Quran and translated a lot of the scriptures into English.

Development of Bengali Language: Raja Ram Mohan Roy considered Bengali prose as a tool for understanding serious philosophical thoughts. He was in favour of a simple, direct styled Bengali prose for the best expression of the best thoughts. Raja Ram Mohan Roy wanted to make Bengali as common people's language, a simple and understandable language by means of which his countrymen would be conscious and concerned about the current problems and happening in surrounding. Raja Ram Mohan Roy wanted to find out one's own root, one's own culture and one's own heritage . So, he wanted to development of Bengali language with English language. He had equal enthusiasm and passion for different vernaculars and wrote a number of tracts in Bengali, Sanskrit and Persian, Hindustani and English. Raja Ram Mohan Roy's Bengali grammar was free from mindless imitation of Sanskrit prose style, because, to him, grammar was not meant to encase a language in a steel frame but to uncover its structure.(Tagore, 1974, pp 60). He wrote Bengali grammar free from heavy complicated Sanskrit language.

He did not copy his grammar from Sanskrit. That was his remarkable contribution and gave the proof of his extraordinary talents of producing Bengali grammar of high order.

Respect for Ancient Language: Raja Ram Mohan Roy had faith in the ancient language and literature of the Hindus. He considered the Sanskrit , as one of the most pure and regularly formed languages of the world. Raja Ram Mohan Roy supported and respected that philosophy of simplicity of life. He believed that true religion and true mentality did not belong to wealth, power, high names and lofty palaces but to simple living and high thinking(Just like Brahmins in ancient time who lived in a small hut, ate simple foods and vegetables, gave education to others) .He believed that the first dawn of knowledge moved upward in the East. That reflects on his book that is "Philosophical and copious language of our own" which makes us distinct from other nations.

But he never mixed up the sentiment with rationality. In his opinion, an ancient language never became progressive for country and for this he had never accepted the proposal of establishing Sanskrit College in Calcutta. He had never accepted anything which could be detrimental to the benefits of his countrymen.

In the field of Literature: The contribution of Ram Mohan Roy in the field of literature was remarkable. He contributed a new style and standard which facilitated the development of Bengali prose as a stories, novels as well as polemical literature. Some Literary Works of Raja Ram Mohan Roy are Tuhfat-ul-Muwahhidin (1804), Vedanta Gantha (1815), Translation of an abridgement of the Vedanta Sara (1816), Kenopanishads (1816), Ishopanishad (1816), Kathopanishad (1817), A Conference between the Advocate for, and an Opponent of Practice of Burning Widows Alive (Bengali and English) (1818), Mundaka Upanishad (1819), A Defence of Hindu Theism (1820), The Precepts of Jesus- The Guide to Peace and Happiness (1820), Bengali Grammar (1826), The Universal Religion (1829), History of Indian Philosophy (1829) and GaudiyaVyakaran (1833).

Women Education: He believed in equality between men and women education. But the cruelty of Sati system was the main barrier. If a girl alive, then only she was able to be educated. Today's generation is much aware about women education. But that time he was the only one who believed that education of girls along with boys only build a progressive society. He believed that with the education of boys, actually a single individual is educated, but with the education of girls, a family is educated. He mentioned the history of highly educated Indian women of Ancient time (From the Vedas).The Brahmo Samaj , founded by him, did great service for women education.

BrahmoSamaj: Raja Ram Mohan Roy founded Brahmo Sabha in 1828, which was later renamed as Brahmo Samaj. It's chief aim was the worship of the eternal God or one god. It was against priesthood, rituals and sacrifices. It focused on prayers, meditation and reading of the scriptures and believed in the unity of all religions. It was the first intellectual reform movement in modern India. It led to the emergence of rationalism and enlightenment in India which indirectly contributed to the nationalist movement.

It split into two in 1866, namely Brahmo Samaj of India led by Keshab Chandra Sen and Adi Brahmo Samaj led by Debendranath Tagore. Some Prominent Leaders of Brahmo Samaj like Debendranath Tagore, Keshab Chandra Sen and Sivnath Shastri helped in women education.

Educational Reforms: He set up several institutions including the Hindu College in Calcutta in 1817, in collaboration with David Hare; the Anglo-Hindu School in 1822 and the Vedanta College, a synthesis of western and Indian learning, in 1826.Raja Ram Mohan Roy set up the Vedanta College to spread his teachings of Hindu monotheism. He promoted the pure ethical Vedanta school of philosophy. He also helped establish the Scottish Church College in 1830. When the government had opened Sanskrit schools, he aimed at promoting subjects like Mathematics, Geography and Latin which, he felt, it were necessary to help the Indians keep pace with the rest of the world. The Hindu College, the City College, Vedanta College, and English Schools all were the result of educational reform of Raja Ram Mohan Roy in Calcutta.

Contribution in the field of journalism: The contribution of Raja Ram Mohan Roy in the field of journalism is remarkable. He started the first Bengali language weekly newspaper and also the first newspaper in an Indian language. His journal, the 'Sambad Kaumudi' that touched upon various topics was very popular. His newspaper 'Sambad Kaumudi' helped people form an opinion about the issues affecting their daily life in British India. In 1822, Roy published the journal 'Mirat-ul-Akhbar' in Persian. Through the efforts of Raja Ram Mohan Roy, Charles Metcalfe removed all the restrictions imposed on Press in 1835 and gave freedom and autonomy to the newspapers in publication and management.

Similarities Among The Ideology Of Raja Ram Mohan Roy And Modern Educational Pattern:

ax. He always supported Modern Liberal Education. As we know that India is a multilingual country, so when people from different regions talk over a single matter, language or dialect barrier creates. But if we all communicate by a common language i. e. English, then it is easier for everyone to participate in that without any hesitation (through a common language). Ram Mohan Roy always supported English Language for education purpose.

ax. Raja Ram Mohan Roy believed to develop the overall education system through establishment of school and colleges were important. So, he established different school and colleges like The Vedanta College, The English School, The City College etc and it helps in the modernization of India.

ax. Besides having the knowledge of different ancient languages like Sanskrit, Persian, Greek, he always supported English as the medium of teaching.

In the modern education system, we also find that many prefers English over other languages.

ax. He was also against the fake prejudices of different religions. The members of Brahmo Samaj believed in one god. Barriers, discrimination among people are result of different religion opinions, Raja Ram Mohan Roy want to remove this barriers by religious universalism.

ax. He was equally and strongly against such other social evils as child-marriage, caste system, polygamy and exploitation of women. He was appalled to see the miserable condition of Hindu widows many of whom were young ladies (Upadhyay, 2008)

ax. His ideas of women education and women empowerment is appreciable.

ax. Newspapers are the Mirror of Society. So he published 'Samvad Kaumudi' and 'Mirat-ul -Akhbar' to propagate his ideas among the people of India.

ax. By writing different books in different languages, he also enriched the literature.

ax. By creating Bengali Prose literature, he also showed his respect toward mother language.

Conclusion: From the above discussion, we understand that, In the area of education, Raja Ram Mohan Roy tackled so many divergent educational problems and programmes with his intellect, sensitivity, perception and compassion. For these qualities Raja Ram Mohan Roy had to face ignorance and many criticism by others. But he was a master mind who only saw that India's progress was dependent only on the self-realisation that isolation from the life of the Western culture and education was only create barriers between east and west. So it was better to accept the west without forgetting our own culture. Raja Ram Mohan Roy was a man who helped us to fight against the superstitions and fake prejudices and guided us to believe in faith and reason.Raja Ram Mohan Roy worked as a pioneer who tirelessly worked for raising his countrymen to a standard from which they could secure honour and prestige for them. He personally made tireless contribution in the field of education directed the attention of government towards a new and enlighten system. After his death ultimately his views regarding liberal education were taken up by Lord Macaulay and supported by Lord Bentinck. So, his educational philosophy, which was the foundations of today's society and it is still significant today.

CHAPTER THIRTEEN

CONTRIBUTIONS OF DR. SARVEPALLI RADHAKRISHNAN

Introduction

"The end-product of education should be a free creative man, who can battle against historical circumstances adversities of nature.-Sarvepalli Radhakrishnan

Sarvepalli Radhakrishnan was an Indian scholar, philosopher, and politician who served as India's first Vice President (1952–1962) and the country's second President (1962–1967). He was born in Tiruttani, Chittoor District, in the erstwhile Madras Presidency, on September 5, 1888. (later in Andhra Pradesh till 1960, now in Tiruvallur district of Tamil Nadu since 1960). Sarvepalli Radhakrishnan was born into a Niyogi Brahmin family who spoke Telugu. Sarvepalli Veeraswami was his father's name, and Sarvepalli Sita was his mother's. His family is from Sarvepalli village in Andhra Pradesh's Nellore district. He spent his early years in Thiruttani and Tirupati. He was a brilliant philosopher, a great teacher, and a Hindu thinker. He was a tutor in India and at Oxford University in the United Kingdom, and was well-known for his work on comparative theology and comparative Eastern and Western philosophy. He was also a statesman who served as India's President. He was a brilliant teacher, and every year on his birthday, September 5th, we all celebrate Teachers Day to honour his contributions to India's educational system. During his lifetime, Radhakrishnan received a knighthood in 1931, the Bharat Ratna, India's highest civilian decoration, in 1954, and honorary membership in the British Royal Order of Merit in 1963. He was also one of the founders of

Helpage India, a non-profit organization dedicated to helping India's elderly and underprivileged.

His primary education was at Thiruttani's K.V High School. In 1896, he transferred to Tirupati's Hermansburg Evangelical Lutheran Mission School and Walajapet's Government High Secondary School. Radhakrishnan spent his life and career as a writer attempting to describe, justify, and propagate his faith, which he referred to variously as Hinduism, Vedanta, and the religion of the Spirit. He wanted to show that his Hinduism was philosophically sound as well as ethically viable. Radhakrishnan has gained the reputation of being a bridge-builder between India and the West because of his concern for experience and thorough understanding of Western intellectual and literary practices. He also seems to be at ease in both Indian and Western metaphysical settings, and he draws on both Western and Indian references in his prose. As a result, Radhakrishnan has been hailed as a leader of Hinduism to the West in scholarly circles. His long literary career and several published works have had a significant impact on how the West views Hinduism, India, and the East.

Major Contributions of Dr. Sarvepalli Radhakrishnan

Radhakrishnan is regarded as one of India's foremost comparative religion and philosophy scholars. His defence of Hinduism against "uninformed Western critique" has had a huge impact in both India and the West. He is also credited with making Hinduism more available to a wider audience in the West.

Education: His services to education and as a national leader will be remembered for a long time. Many young people have been motivated by his work and accomplishments. Radhakrishnan defines education as the acquisition of skills outside the academic and technical realms. He believed that education should not be limited to bookish schooling or the memorization of statistics and figures, nor should it be used to fill the mind with useless knowledge. It is therefore not the memorization of others' thoughts and their reproduction in tests to obtain diplomas and degrees for jobs.

Education is the process of assimilating ideals and concepts in order to develop character and prepare for life's challenges. According to Radhakrishnan, where scientific knowledge ends, the realm of mystery begins. The worlds of scientific reality and morals are not the same. All of education's technical, science, and technological achievements will be worthless until it instills knowledge and humanity in men's hearts and minds. Education is a spiritual awakening that clears the mind and illuminates the personality. In his soft, kind-hearted, open, energetic, and loving approach, a teacher must build an atmosphere that nurtures the pupil. He must instills a sense of leadership in his students by allowing them to take on leadership positions.

In the classroom, reciprocal understanding between teacher and student can foster a positive and constructive atmosphere. Students may feel safe to share their emotions and learn to appreciate and listen to others if their thoughts and views are valued. New training tactics should not be feared by the teacher. He must prioritize collaborative decision-making, collaboration, and community growth.

We all know that Dr. Sarvepalli Radhakrishnan was one of India's greatest and most illustrious philosophers, as well as a renowned and diplomatic teacher. Because of Dr. Sarvepalli Radhakrishnan's contributions to education, his birthday is commemorated as Teachers Day on September 5th across the world. This is because Radhakrishnan's students wanted him to give him an allowance to celebrate his birthday, so he told all of his students that this day should be celebrated as Teacher's Day.

"Instead of celebrating my birthday, it would be my proud privilege if 5 September is observed as Teachers' Day."- Dr. Sarvepalli Radhakrishnan.

This day honour not only Dr. Sarvepalli Radhakrishnan, but all teachers who have contributed to and continue to contribute to the field of education. His commitment to the Indian country is enormous and lasting. He was a wonderful and well-liked educator who saw education's challenges from the ground up. His paper, titled "University Commission, 1948-49," informs us of his educational theories and is considered the most significant contribution to education.

The curriculum must be relevant to everyday life. Languages, Literature, Social Studies (Geography, History, Economics, etc.), Philosophy, Ethics, Theology, Morality, Politics, Civics, Science (Natural, Human, etc.), Mathematics, Art/Music/Fine Arts, Vocation / Profession Subjects (Agriculture, Law, Medicine, Trade and Commerce, Home Science, Typewriting, Poultry, Dairy farming, Shoemaking, etc.), Mathematics, Art/Music/Fine Arts.

In 1946, he was appointed ambassador to UNESCO, and then to the Soviet Union. He was instrumental in laying the groundwork for India's alliance with the Soviet Union (now Russia). During the Cold War, he served as India's second ambassador to Moscow from 1949 to 1953. He was in charge of India's alliance with the Soviet Union at the time. During the meeting, Stalin said that clapping requires two hands and that the Cold War was caused by a third party. Then, Radhakrishnan replied, "As a peace-loving country, the Soviet Union should withdraw its own hand as it takes two hands to clap".

Radhakrishnan was dubbed "a living bridge between the East and the West" by American educator Paul Artue Schillip because he gracefully translated Indian thinking into western words. He demonstrated to the rest of the world that Indian ideas are rational and logical.

He also received the Bharat Ratna in 1954, was knighted by George V in 1931 for his contributions to education, and was given honorary membership in the British Royal Order of Merit in 1963. Dr. Radhakrishnan was unafraid to speak out on national and international topics. In 1965, he suggested a proposal for peace in Vietnam that included both sides withdrawing and the country being administered by an Asian African police force before the Vietnamese could form their own government.

In June 1926, Radhakrishnan led the University of Calcutta at the British Empire Universities Congress, and in September 1926, he attended the International Congress of Philosophy at Harvard University. Radhakrishnan was invited to Manchester College, Oxford, in 1929 to fill the vacancy left by Principal J. Estlin Carpenter (now Harris-Manchester College). This gave him the chance to give a Comparative Religion lecture to University of Oxford students.

In Europe and the United States, his translations of classic Hindu texts and thinkers were widely read, leading to the kind of understanding that was one of his main goals.

Dr. Sarvepalli Radhakrishnan was a brilliant scholar and statesman who served as India's first Vice-President and second President. He was a well-known academician and scholar. The Vice-Chancellor of Calcutta University welcomed Sarvepalli Radhakrishnan to become a Professor of Mental and Moral Science. In Calcutta, he had a close relationship with Rabindranath Tagore. He was so taken by the Nobel Laureate's philosophy that he decided to write his first book on him. He'd also given talks at Manchester College and the Haskell Institute in Chicago. He has worked at Oxford University as the Spalding Professor of Eastern Religions. In 1962, he was elected President of India. Bertrand Russel greeted him upon his appointment as President of India. Dr. Sarvepalli Radhakrishnan was a brilliant teacher and a person who led India through difficult times. India was at war with both China and Pakistan when he became President. He had previously served as vice-chancellor of Andhra University and Banaras University. In 1921, he was promoted to India's most prestigious philosophy chair.

During his lifetime, Radhakrishnan received several honour, including five consecutive nominations for the Nobel Prize in Literature. However, he was never awarded the Nobel Prize. He also received the Bharat Ratna in 1954, was knighted by George V in 1931 for his contributions to education, and was given honorary membership in the British Royal Order of Merit in 1963. He was the first person to receive the Sahitya Akademi fellowship, the Sahitya Akademi's highest honor bestowed on a novelist, in 1968. He was awarded the Templeton Prize for spreading the concept of "a divine truth of God that promoted love and knowledge for all mankind" shortly before his death in 1975. Sir Sarvepalli Radhakrishnan was knighted in 1931, and he was known as Sir Sarvepalli Radhakrishnan until India's independence in 1947; after that, he was known as Dr. Sarvepalli Radhakrishnan. He was also awarded the German Book Trade's Peace Prize.

Social contributions

One more astonishing fact about him is that after becoming the President of India, he remained a humble man. He only accepted Rs 2500 out of his salary Rs 10,000 and donated the remaining amount to the Prime Minister's National Relief Fund every month. He had also formed the Krishnarpan Charity Trust along with Ghanshyam Das Birla and some other social workers in the pre-independence era. His philosophy was based on Advaita Vedanta, which he reinterpreted for a modern audience. He contributed to the development of contemporary Hindu identity by defending Hinduism against what he termed "uninformed Western critique."

Radhakrishnan's defence of Hindu values has had a huge impact, both in India and in the West. Radhakrishnan's thoughts aided in the establishment of India as a nation-state in India. Radhakrishnan's writings led to Vedanta's hegemonic position as "Hinduism's basic world view." Radhakrishnan's representations of Hindu tradition in the western world, as well as his focus on "spiritual experience," made Hinduism more available to a western audience and led to Hinduism's impact on western spirituality. He was opposed to state agencies providing denominational religious education because it went against the Indian state's secular vision. Theology and creeds are intellectual formulations and symbols of divine knowledge, or "religious intuitions," for Radhakrishnan. Radhakrishnan ranked the various religions according to their perception of "holy knowledge," with Advaita Vedanta occupying the highest position:

- The worshippers of the Absolute
- The worshippers of the personal God
- The worshippers of the incarnations like Rama, Krishna, Buddha
- Those who worship ancestors, deities and sages
- The worshippers of the petty forces and spirits

Hinduism, according to Radhakrishnan, is a logical faith founded on reality that can be grasped by intuition or religious experience. "If philosophy of religion is to become science, it must become analytical and based on religious knowledge," says Radhakrishnan. Due to his vast intelligence, he was the bridge-builder between East and West. He has the potential to break down abstract concepts into simple terms. Dr. Radhakrishnan was critical of how Western philosophers taught. The critique was based on the belief that theology controlled western thinkers, restricting freedom of speech. He published books on Indian philosophy that met Western scholarly expectations, and he worked tirelessly to get the West to take Indian philosophy seriously. He contrasts various ways of thinking processes in his novel, Idealist View of Life, and favors the simplified logical approach. He is well-known for his study of the human way of life by listening to elders (Upanishads), using common sense (Brahma Sutra), and behaving in a rational manner (Bhagavat Gita).

His works include The Philosophy of Rabindranath Tagore, Living with a Reason, Hindu Philosophy, The Pursuit of Truth, Upanishad Philosophy, Eastern Religions among Western Thought, and others.

In 1975, he won the Templeton Prize for promoting the notion of "a universal reality of God that embraced love and wisdom for all people". He had donated his entire prize money to Oxford University. In the memory of Dr. Radhakrishnan Oxford University has set up a scholarship known as "Radhakrishnan Chevening Scholarship". Dr. Sarvepalli Radhakrishnan has given his valuable contribution in international journals this man given many great educational books and articles to the Indian nation.

He wrote many books in his whole lifetime and some famous books are Indian Philosophy, The Pursuit of Truth, The Hindu View of Life, The Philosophy of Rabindranath Tagore, The Bhagavad-Gita, The Dhammapada, Religion and Culture, The Brahma Sutra: The Philosophy of Spiritual Life, and many more. Dr. Radhakrishnan was an idealist philosopher. He was an advocate of ancient Indian Vedanta Philosophy. This is clear from his works „The Hindu View of Life", Brahma sutra. An idealist View of Life". As for as spirit is concerned, Radhakrishnan's philosophy is mysticism. In his book „An idealist View of Life", he has called spirit-total Brahman. Radhakrishnan was a powerful advocate for Indian religion and culture. His writing was apologetic to some extent, reacting to Western critiques of Hinduism as a negative social power, citing the caste system and women's status as examples. He interacted with Western philosophy in an innovative way, showing that Eastern thought deserved equal academic recognition and that it complemented Western philosophy. He promoted theological peace and concord and stood for the unification of the human spirit. When he became President of India, some of his classmates and friends asked him if they could celebrate his birthday, September 5, with him. He suggested that instead of celebrating the occasion, it would be better if it be observed as Teacher's Day. Since then, the day has been dedicated to teachers.

Conclusion

Therefore, we can conclude that, Dr. Sarvepalli Radhakrishnan was an excellent teacher and a wonderful human being. Thanks to his vast intelligence, he was the bridge-builder between East and West. He was a tutor in India and at Oxford University in the United Kingdom, and was well-known for his work on comparative theology and comparative Eastern and Western philosophy. He was also a statesman who served as India's President. He was a well-known academician and scholar. He was an excellent teacher, and in recognition of his valuable contributions to India's educational system, every year on his birthday, September 5th, we all commemorate Teachers Day to honour our teachers who serve as a guiding light in our lives. He'd received a number of coveted prizes and titles. He served as India's ambassador to UNESCO and was awarded the Bharat Ratna. On April 17, 1975, Dr. Sarvepalli Radhakrishnan, a scholar and statesman who served as President and Vice President of India, died.

CHAPTER FOURTEEN

CONTRIBUTION OF ISHWAR CHANDRA VIDYASAGAR

Introduction

Ishwar chandra vidyasagar was one of the greatest reformers born in India in the nineteenth century. He was the symbol of the Bengal renaissance. He had a wonderful combination of European renaissance rationalism, secularism, intense humanism, and eastern and western ideologies. Ishwar chandra vidyasagar was one of the best education reformers in our subcontinent. vidyasagar's role in the introduction of widow marriage and the prevention of child marriage is not as well known as his contribution to education reform. In fact, just as Raja Rammohan Roy played a role in building a modern society in this country, Vidyasagar can be called a pioneer in reforming our education system.

There is no one who has not heard the name of Ishwar Chandra Vidyasagar's as a Bengali. He is equally popular in both east and west Bengal. The main reason for his popularity was his work on education. Ishwar Chandra Vidyasagar's took a far-reaching aspect of Raja Rammohan Roy's education reform. Raja Rammohan was the pioneer of modern society in bengal, and then Ishwar Chandra Vidyasagar's took the responsibility of educating in modern education. We can discuss Vidyasagar's contribution in the context of bengali social movement in the context of education reform and social reform.

Vidyasagar's role in Education Reform:

Vidyasagar's was multilingualism. He wanted to reformed the education system of Bengali society in such a way that every person in Bengal could become educated. He was appointed as the principal of Sanskrit college. The changes he made to the administration and the academy during his tenure as head of the institution were unprecedented. The most important part of his proposed and formulated education system is to eradicate prejudice from the society.

Inspired by deep humanism, Vidyasagar was a novice in the spread of education from the very beginning. He wanted to make the academy a nursery of human religion, the important steps he took to spread education were as follows:

Establishment of schools: Vidyasagar was the first to emphasize on the establishment of schools in the field of education reform. When Lord Hardinge insisted on establishing 100 bengali schools in 1844, Vidyasagar extended a helping hand to him. Not only that, he himself established 20 model schools in different districts, most of which was run at his own expense. He also established the "Metropolitan institution" at his own expense in 1872, now known as Vidyasagar college.

The role of women's education: Vidyasagar understood that if women could not be educated in the society then women could not make overall progress. That is why women became enterprising in the spread of education. He founded the Hindu female school under the auspices of Drink water Bethune, and also associated himself with the establishment of 35 girls' schools , about 1300 students were studying in the schools.

Teaching in mother tongue: Vidyasagar had emphasized on teaching in mother tongue from the very beginning but at the same time he did not deny the importance of western education. At the same time, he emphasized the importance of combining east and west.

Making rules and regulations in the field of education: He established a number of rules for teaching. He opened the door to study Sanskrit for Hindu students of all castes by upholding position of the principle in that time only **Brahmin** and **Vaidya** children could study Sanskrit. He also enforced some new rules in the college like stopping teachers from coming and going as they wished. Besides, he introduced the holiday rule on Sunday by lifting the holiday according to the auspicious day. Not only did he become Vidyasagar himself through education, he wanted every person in the society to be educated in higher education. He wanted girls to be educated in higher education and make themselves equal to men. In that case he has got special success. For this reason, the role of Vidyasagar in the education reform of Bengal and India cannot be denied.

Vidyasagar's Education Reform:

Modernize and update textbooks: A major factor in the modernization of textbooks is that case Vidyasagar's was a staunch supporter of mother tongue education. He had a deep faith in the power inherent in the Bengali language and he wanted to make the Bengali language useful by keeping that faith in mind. He tried to modernize the Bengali alphabet by freeing it from the complex rules of Sanskrit grammar. He freed Bengali from the entanglement of Sanskrit and transformed Bengali into a scientific language. His **"Byakaron kaumudi"** bears the signature of vidyasagar's efforts. Similarly, he became a novice in the reform of the Bengali script. In 1874, his essay **"Barnaparichay"** was published. The script he reformed in this book later became the standard of Bengali script. The book is still equally popular after half a year and the script is still in use in Bengali.

Ensuring secularism in the education structure: He wanted to free education from the shackles of religion and make it secular, secular and scientific. Vidyasagar was a scholar of Hindu scriptures but still he did not hesitate to abandon religion from the field of education. He was always been a reformer in the field of education. With a modern mindset, he sought to establish the structure of education on secular liberal grounds. He wanted to free the education system from the shackles of religious education and bring it in line with western education. Vidyasagar's line of thought initiated the philosophy of liberal secular education. His textbooks are also a shining example of his secular consciousness. Vidyasagar was science-minded in thought and consciousness. So he was particularly interested in the development of science education and the introduction of scientific thought. His writings and works show signs of his love of science. There was still enthusiasm for various scientific theories and discoveries.

Establishment and expansion of educational institutions for the expansion of education, especially women's education: Vidyasagar always wanted education to spread and every person in Bengal to be educated. So he was an enterprising man in establishing schools in the villages. He set up unpaid schools in various places so that poor students could study without pay. The main objective is to ensure that the benefits of education are not limited to the affluent society but extend to the poor. He sincerely believed that high quality education was not only a monopoly of the west but also of Indian teachers. Great evidence of the Metropolitan Institute he established in 1972, now called Vidyasagar College.

One of the works of Vidyasagar in the spread of education is the spread of women's education. He believed that the advancement of women was far-reaching in the overall development of different countries and nations. It was on his initiative that the Calcutta Hindu girls 'school was established the first girls' school in India. Later it was known as Bethune school. While in Sanskrit college, he sat down to do a job that required a strong mindset and refuted very intelligent reasoning. He opened the Sanskrit college to all. There was no barrier to study or go there for any religion, racism or personality of any particular religious ideology. During the nineteenth century, such acts were considered as atheism and blasphemy in Bengal. Blasphemy is those who have a disrespectful attitude towards god. He first started taking admission fees and tuition fees in sanskrit colleges. Strictly emphasizing punctuality and discipline, he introduced the first weekly vacation. After joining Sanskrit college, Vidyasagar converted Sanskrit into Bengali and used them as text. The rationale behind this was that students could easily select any subject written in Sanskrit and read according to their choice. He started a practice of taking tests. His focus was not only on Sanskrit education but also on English, western science and mathematics.

Vidyasagar started taking monthly examinations of educational institutions. This is another proof of his foresight. He started the system of continuous comprehensive evaluation of colleges and universities 200 years ago. He realized that if students were to take exams all year round instead of just one exam a year, students would be in reading all year long. Knowing that it is important to understand the importance of education to build a better society, he explained in advance. Vidyasagar's was a philanthropist but that is not all he has done for the betterment of his own Sanskrit college. Satisfied with his work, the government appointed him an inspector in various schools in Bengal. After being appointed inspector, he established about 20 schools in four districts. Not only did he set up schools but he also took charge of them, developed modern syllabus and called for teachers. Not only did he create the whole learning context in a new way, he also created teachers. He knew that those who would teach the new syllabus would not be familiar with such an education system, so he recommended that a separate school be set up with each school to train them properly, so that teachers could be properly trained.

Ishwar Chandra Vidyasagar was not limited to the expansion of education. The main purpose of the students is to study and apply that study in their field of work. He took this matter very seriously so he recommended to the government that job arrangements and opportunities be created for the students after passing and he was very successful.

Conclusion: From the above discussion it is understood how far Ishwar Chandra Vidyasagar's was ahead as a human being. He has educated himself and has taken up the work of educating others as a profession. He has worked tirelessly to educate and build the society. He has worked all his life to make everyone understand the importance of education and to build an educated society. Sometimes it happens that there is no book for teaching anywhere, he has arranged the book there at his own expense. He had a task above all else and that was to bring the light of education in the society and to make the society educated. The humanist Vidyasagar's expressed his ideal thinking through the philosophy of education. His approach to education was very pragmatic. Although he was a Sanskrit scholar and a scholar of the scriptures, he sought to free education from the influence of spirituality which characterized his secular character. His activities in Sanskrit college show that the right to education is universal. It is not right to restrict education to any one class. Again, the combination of eastern and western education, the spread of education shows his generosity. His generosity in setting up schools and widow marriages at his own expense to enlighten superstitious people in the light of education is a testament to his generosity. The marginalized class of the society thought of the Santhals which is constitutionally recognized today. Above all, he will be immortalized forever in his famous book **'Barnaparichay'**. So in the end we cannot deny that Vidyasagar's contribution to our lives is deeply rooted in the 21st century.

CHAPTER FIFTEEN

APJ ABDUL KALAM'S EDUCATIONAL PHILOSOPHY

Introduction

Thinking should become your capital asset, no matter whatever ups and downs you come across in your life. -APJ Abdul Kalam

Dr. APJ Abdul Kalam is a well-known name in the world. He is regarded as one of the most brilliant scientists of the twenty-first century. Furthermore, he becomes India's 11th president and serves his country. He was the country's most cherished citizen because of his incomparable contributions as a scientist and a president. Apart from that, he has made a significant contribution to the Indian Space Research Organization (ISRO). He was in charge of a number of projects that benefited society, and he was also involved in the production of the Agni and Prithvi missiles. He was dubbed "India's Missile Man" because of his interest in nuclear power. Dr. APJ Abdul Kalam wrote several books during his lifetime, but his most notable work was 'India 2020,' which contains an action plan to make India a superpower. Dr. APJ Abdul Kalam was a straightforward and honest man. He was so preoccupied with his job that he would get up early in the morning and work until late at night. With his favourite slogan, "strength respects strength," Kalam justifies India's nuclear weapons. Why we should be concerned about India's few nuclear weapons when there are 10,000 nuclear warheads on the other side of the Atlantic, he says. Kalam's coworkers believe that his philosophical bent of mind has aided him in mastering the art of achieving consensus. He still sets his sights high. When asked about his reaction to being given the presidency, the man, still overcome by the realisation that someone from humble beginnings like him can hold the highest office in the world, is ecstatic at the wonderful vagaries of Indian polity. He could only say gleefully to the waiting media, "It feels fantastic."

"Books become permanent companions. Sometimes, they are born before us; they guide us during our life journey and continue for many generations."

Kalam's concept of Education

According to Dr. A.P.J Abdul Kalam, education has a huge role to play in transforming a child into a leader—the shift from "what can you do for me?" to "what can you do for you?" The most crucial aspect of education is instilling in students the belief that "we can do it." Education is a never-ending search for wisdom and enlightenment. True education raises a person's integrity and self-esteem, and universal brotherhood in its true sense becomes the bedrock of such education. The following are the most pressing educational issues in the majority of the world's nations.

ax.   To correlate education with the problems of life.

ax.   To democratize education.

ax.   To cope with the problems arising out of the modern scientific and technical advancement.

ax.   To make education adequately efficient.

Education, according to Dr. APJ Abdul Kalam, is about bringing out and improving students' innate imagination. Every Indian boy, according to Dr. Kalam, has a fundamental right to education. Dr. Kalam considers education to be the most important aspect of the service sector because it offers the necessary expertise and skills to perform any task.

Dr. Kalam's Perspective aims on Education

"Education is the cornerstone to ensure the development of enlightened people who will make a prosperous, peaceful, and strong country," says Dr. Kalam. "When learning is purposeful, imagination blooms, and when creativity blooms, thinking emanates," he says. When Thinking shines brightly, Knowledge shines brightly as well. When the light of information is turned on, the economy thrives."

According to Dr. Kalam, the educational system can keep children's smiles. This is possible if the educational system is made more innovative throughout and everyone is given full employment. The following are Dr. Kalam's key educational goals:

ax.   To help students develop character and human values.

ax.   Infuse imagination and foster a scientific mindset with

ax.   To use technology to improve learning ability.

ax.   To instil hope in children in order for them to face the future.

ax.   To ensure the development of enlightened people in order for the country to be stable, happy, and strong.

ax.   To help students improve their analysis and inquiry skills.

ax.   To show off one's innovative abilities and entrepreneurial spirit.

ax.   To establish moral leadership.

ax.   To make the country energy self-sufficient.

To instil in students a sense of integrity, self-respect, and self-reliance.

Kalam's thought on Children

Dr. Abdul Kalam claimed that each child is born with certain inherited characteristics, into a particular socioeconomic and emotional context, and is taught in specific ways by authority figures. When children grow older, they should be given chances to replicate such good acts in order to instil good behaviours in them. These positive behaviours will serve them well in the future.The first years of a person's life are formative and therefore vital to their growth. Dr. Abdul Kalam saw India's children as the country's future, and he was always concerned about the growing number of atrocities committed against them. "It is easier to build strong children than to fix damaged adults," writes Dr. Abdul Kalam. According to Dr. Abdul Kalam, today's people may not thrive in the future, but today's children are expected to. If today's children are moulded in their attitudes, beliefs, thoughts, and morals, we may expect a stronger and more structured world tomorrow. And we have the ability to realise our current vision for the future.

Curriculum: The curriculum, according to Dr. Abdul Kalam, should be focused on science and technology. There should be space for expression, as well as opportunities to try new things and learn by doing. Curriculum must include the development of morals, compassion, discipline, cooperation, nonviolence, religious peace, spiritualism, imagination, and faith in God. Entrepreneurial and management skills should be taught alongside other subjects.

Role of Teachers: "Teaching is a very noble profession that shapes the character, calibre, and future of a count," says Dr. Abdul Kalam. The school teacher has a significant role to play in shaping the character of the student, especially during the adolescent years. Dr. Kalam writes that it would be the greatest honour for him if people recognise him as a good teacher. There is no profession in the world, according to Dr. Abdul Kalam, that is more important to society than teaching. Teachers are a country's backbone, the foundation upon which all aspirations are transformed into realities.

According to Dr. Abdul Kalam, teachers must play an important role in students' learning. He claims that learning necessitates the ability to visualise, and that both must be encouraged by the teacher. Dr. Abdul Kalam emphasises the importance of teacher planning. He claims that a successful instructor prepares himself for teaching and the student for knowledge acquisition by careful preparation. Dr. Abdul Kalam writes about the teacher's sacrifice. He writes that the teacher's position is akin to the proverbial "ladder": everybody uses it to climb up in life, but the ladder itself remains in place.

Role of Parents: Dr. APJ Abdul Kalam believed that every parent should teach their children how to be good human beings. He writes that it is important for every parent to be able to make the effort to teach their children how to be enlightened and hardworking human beings. Abdul Kalam believes that parents should encourage their children to dream. Success still follows the realisation of dreams, though there might be some failures and delays along the way. Parents and teachers, according to Dr. Kalam, play a significant role in the lives of children. He claims that if parents and teachers devote themselves to shaping the lives of children, India will be given a new lease on life. As the saying goes, "the school is behind the parents, and the home is behind the teacher."

The Educational thoughts of Dr. APJ Abdul Kalam

Education is a never-ending search for wisdom and enlightenment. The focus of education and schools must be on mission-oriented learning that is based on a value system. Childhood is the cornerstone upon which the entire life structure is built, as the seeds planted in childhood develop into the tree of life. Education provided to children at any point of their mental development is more critical than education obtained in college and university. Education fosters a child's interest in the world and combines the thought process with hand, limb, and body skills. To create an open and transparent society, twelve years of value-based education on the school campus are required. Exploration, innovation, and imagination should be emphasised through activities. Experiments, problem solving, and teamwork should be emphasised at the secondary level. Bio-info-nano-eco education should be converged at all stages of education.

Conclusion: In the country, Dr. APJ Abdul Kalam is known as the missile kid. He was a scientist who rose to become India's 11th president, but he aspired to be recognised as a teacher, as he writes. Learning, he writes, is a lifelong practise. The educated are those who know others, but the wise are those who know themselves. It's pointless to learn if you don't have any wisdom. "It would be presumptuous to suggest that my life can be a role model for anyone," writes Dr. Abdul Kalam, "but some poor child living in a remote location in an underprivileged social setting will find some solace in the way my destiny has been shaped."Dr. Kalam was a great inspiration to many people, especially children, who he encouraged to dream big and accomplish great things in life. He voiced his opinions on every aspect of education, as we have seen. Dr. APJ Abdul Kalam belongs in the company of great educational thinkers. "Dr. Abdul Kalam's wonderful thoughts are a perfect perspective for all. It can be used by instructors, entrepreneurs, coaches, corporate mentors and executives, and everyone else who is mentoring and teaching someone or a team to go beyond boundaries and achieve greatness."

Dr. Abdul Kalam focused his remarks on two key topics: education and information technology. India is currently focusing on these two sectors, which are both growing in terms of jobs. As a result, both our curriculum and information technology are rapidly evolving. Kalam's dream is about to come true, and India's youth are playing a critical role in its growth.

CHAPTER SIXTEEN

EDUCATIONAL PHILOSOPHIES OF JOHN LOCKE

Introduction

At the very beginning of *Some Thoughts Concerning Education* John Locke signals his view of the importance of the subject: "I think I may say that of all the men we meet with, nine parts of ten are what they are, good or evil, useful or not, by their education. It's that which makes the great difference in mankind."Locke's assessment of the formative role of education is hardly surprising given the deeply egalitarian premises of his natural rights philosophy in his seminal political writing *The Two Treatises of Government*. Here Locke grounded natural rights on the basic human equality derived from our status as being "promiscuously born to the same faculties" (Locke 1988: II, 4). In this context he affirmed that the ultimate goal of education is rational autonomy and the full independence of children upon reaching maturity: "Age and Reason as they grow up, loosen them [the Bonds of Subjection] till at length they quite drop off, and leave a Man at his own free Disposal" (Locke 1988: II, 55). Natural freedom and equality thus are the core philosophical ideas underlying Locke's teaching on education. Yet as several commentators have observed, there are two aspects of Locke's argument in the *Thoughts* that seem to conflict, or be in tension, with the egalitarian premises of his natural rights philosophy. First, Locke directs his ideas in the *Thoughts* not at all children, but rather primarily for the sons of well-to-do gentlemen (Horwitz 1986: 141). Second, Locke's recommendations seem to presuppose that a proper education can only take place in the private family under the instruction of a personal tutor (Tarcov 1984: 3-4). Together these propositions suggest that Locke had a narrowly class-based conception of education that in practice had little application to the public more generally. This chapter reexamines the role of the public in Locke's educational writings. Contrary to the notion that Locke's educational theory focused on the requirements of a particular social class, this study will argue that Locke's educational writings were permeated with an acute sensitivity to the importance of education as a public good. Indeed, Locke's educational theory aimed at nothing less than formulating the intellectual basis of a conception of democratic citizenship for Lockean liberal society. In order to illuminate the central role of the public in Locke's thoughts on education, it is necessary to examine his understanding of the multiple dimensions of what is public. This multifarious idea of the public is only intelligible; however, if we look beyond the *Thoughts* and include in our analysis his other major educational writings, the later *conduct of the Understanding* and his "Essay on the Poor Law."Takenin their totality, these writings presenta comprehensive treatment of education designed to suit the requirements of various stages of individual development and maturity. Perhaps the most revolutionary, but rarely noticed, aspect of Locke's educational writings, spanning early childhood education in the *Thoughts* to a call for reform of university curricula in the *Conduct*, is his foreshadowing of contemporary approaches to education that integrate pre-school, primary, secondary, higher education and continuing education. Each aspect of Locke's educational proposals includes an important public dimension and element of liberal democratic citizenship. In a sense, this culminates in his plan to institute his key pedagogical insights in a system of publicly funded "work schools" for poor children which would have made providing educational opportunity on a massive scale a legitimate public policy objective arguably for the first time in history. This paper proceeds in three sections. In section one, we consider Locke's account of the importance of socialization in early education and the training in moral virtues Locke sees as the natural corollary of proper socialization. These are fundamentally democratic virtues designed to deepen the individual's egalitarian sympathies, while simultaneously preparing for rational autonomy upon maturity. Section two turns to Locke's treatment of higher education in the *Conduct* and his recommendations for producing an informed citizenry, open to rationaldiscourse and scientific advance. The final section examines Locke's argument in the "Essay on the Poor Law" for the extensive use of public power to promote education as a societal goal, which he insists will not only enhance the "welfare and prosperity of the nation" by making more rational citizens. It also promises to support the individual reflection upon the issues of politics, religion and science that comprises the very essence of democratic citizenship in Lockean liberal society. Locke's opinion, the way in which contemporary (17th-century) English young ladies are learning French – without a help of a written gram-mar, only through contact with the spoken language of their *bones* and their use of language in everyday life – is much more useful and natural than that of a young gentlemen who are learning Latin from books in organized lessons and use it only for reading and writing books. Locke's unique thoughts on differences between the ways in which ladies and gentlemen are learning foreign languages are not the most original part of his "system" of ideas on education. Locke's main original contribution is a new attitude towards abilities and possibilities of human beings, which is connected to his thoughts in epistemology, political philosophy, and theology. If I am to briefly outline these connections in Locke's curve, I can say: our minds are *tabulate resale* from his epistemological point of view, we are freeborn human beings as citizens from the point of view of his political philosophy, and we are free from original sin according to his theology. These statements are three faces of the same hidden anthropology, which appears in its clearest form on pages of Locke's educational work.

Introduction of John Locke

John Lockemade significant contributions to the History ofModern Philosophy in both epistemology and political theory. Though Descartes wanted to provide a solid, indubitable foundation for knowledge, Locke viewed Rationalism s resting upon still unquestioned assumptions, like the assumption that the mind is born with ideas at birth, and the further assumption that clarity of concepts can give accurate knowledge of reality. Locke reasoned that it was important to begin with a better awareness of the limitations of human knowledge before engaging in metaphysical speculation. In the introduction to *An Essay Concerning Human Understanding* Locke unveils this critical agenda in setting out to inquire into the "extent of human knowledge." In the first section of the book Locke (not included in this selection) Locke refutes Descartes' notion of innate ideas. Then, at the start of the second book, (included in this selection) Locke establishes the starting point of Empiricism. There are thus no innate ideas; all ideas originate in the mind through experience, through either sensation or reflection upon the ideas obtained through sensation. Locke begins by making a distinction between ideas in the mind and the qualities of bodies which the ideas are supposed to resemble. Locke's argument is that the ideas of secondary qualities, which are constantly changing, cannot thus be accurate resemblances of the unchanging substance. Only the ideas of *primary qualities* can thus be true resemblances of the things themselves. Locke puts forth a *causal theory of perception* in which the primary qualities of sometimes even imperceptible bodies press upon the sense organs leaving impressions that would make their way through the mechanism of the body to become ideas in the mind. Locke's epistemology provided the starting point for Empiricism, but it certainly did not solve the fundamental problem of knowledge set up by Descartes. The problem with Locke's argument would be revealed by his immediate Empiricist successor, George Berkeley.

Interpretations of Locke's educational writings

Before the analysis of Locke's text, I have to make some methodological notes. Margaret Ezell, a historian of the 18th-century education, noted: "Leibniz, it was reported, considered it [Locke's *Some Thoughts Concerning Education*] a more important work than *An Essay Concerning Human Understanding*, and it went through several editions in French, German, Italian,Dutch, and Swedish during the eighteenth century." (Ezzel, 1991, 237). Ezzel, according to the *Checklist of Printings* of the Cambridge critical edition of Locke's booklet (Locke, 1968, 98–104), did not mention any Central-European edition. Later, in the second half of the 20th century, a year after the publication of the abovementioned critical edition, a representative volume of researches on Locke, edited by John W. Yolton, discussed all aspects of philosophy of Locke; however without any note regarding his booklet on education (Yolton, 1969). More than a decade later, John Dunn, a well-known researcher of Locke and his time, gave only a passing comment on this booklet in his small but wide-reaching monograph on Locke. In a striking contrast to this ignorance of the historians of philosophy, Locke's educational work was always appreciated in the fields of history of ideas and history of education. Researches in those fields can provide new and interesting insights on connections between Locke's work and the contemporary genre of *courtesy book* as well as on Locke's influence on the perception of childhood as it was presented in the 18th-century English and French novels (e.g. Fielding's *Tom Jones* and Rousseau's *Emil*). The history of Locke's reception, especially in France and Germany, has been by now thoroughly investigated. For ex-ample, the research on the relations between thoughts on education of Locke and those of Christian Wolff is nowadays almost a separate field of research in historiography (for an early example see: Brown, 1952). These are very interesting fields of research; however scholars rarely expand their research efforts to finding the correct place of Locke's work on education in his overall system of thoughts. Only a few authors have offered their hypotheses on the role which the small work *Some Thoughts Concerning Education* might have in Locke's curve. Those writers were mainly interested in Locke's anthropological views, so their inquiries were focused on recovering or reconstructing Locke's hidden anthropology. In Locke's booklet they wanted to find what they have not found in an explicit form in his great academic works (e.g. in his *Essay*). In those works, Locke's anthropology is connected to theological anthropology of a particular Christian denomination and strongly linked with some speculative thoughts on Locke's personal faith, expressed within a denominational conceptual framework. Tendencies to describe Locke's writings in religious terms are especially visible in British work on Locke and his origins, and are being followed by contemporary researchers of Locke as well. Good example is Canadian philosopher David Gauthier who put the religious questions in Locke-interpretations at the central place when he defined Locke's thinking as "theocentric" (Gauthier, 1977). One should have an overview before sinking into the depths of religious interpretations of Locke.

Approach of history of education

Religious approach discussed above poses a question on the relation between Locke's *Some Thoughts Concerning Education* and John Milton's work *Of Education* in terms of development of Locke's position towards education. Milton had an influence on Locke's opinions on politics and other questions of society – the influence of Milton's *Areopagitica* on Locke's *Epistle on Toleration* is well-known – and thereligious content is more explicit in his works. (Milton, 1991, 227). In his interpretation of Locke's *Essay*, W.M. Spellman adds an explication of Locke's educational booklet (Spellman, 1991). Spellman within this framework argues against the novelty of Locke's thoughts on education: "In fact, there is a very little in the work to suggest that the author was breaking new and controversial ground in the area of educational theory." (Spellman, 1991, 207). Spellman's clear aim is to re-link Locke to the mainstream tradition of early modern Protestant thinking. He believes that Locke's sentences on "blank slate", "white paper", and "tabula rasa" is overestimated in modern interpretations. Spellman emphasizes strong Locke's *loci* on the weakness of human minds and traces them back to the well-known Christian doctrine which views every human being as a creature of God. Spellman writes: "Milton's [above quoted] conviction [...on] education was [...] Locke's conviction as well" (Spellman, 1991, 221). In my opinion, one can interpret Milton's words as a sign of Pelagian or Unitarian anthropology with perfectible human beings and without original sin as well. Instead of talking about human nature in general, she speaks about "human nature embodied in a new-born child" which, according to authors of early modern educational theories, can be innately evil, innately good, or "blank". Ezell is not interested in theological consequences; she focuses mainly on earthly circumstances of the educational theory. That was the reason why she considered Mil-ton's and Locke's aims of education as opposed to each other: Milton's end is heavenly, while Locke's end is earthly endeavor. Alex Neill wrote more serious and unbiased analysis of the role of education in Locke's system of ideas (Neill, 1991). Neill believes that without Locke's booklet on education we could not resolve important contradiction in his anthropology. Neill's suggestion is: "A good education, then, fosters autonomy and virtue through habituating the child to self-mastery; however, involves habituating the child to reason." (Neill, 1991, 256).

Central-European reception of Locke's theory of education

Every researcher should have no problems in finding Locke-editions in European languages that are omitted from the list. The interpretation of Locke-reception in the so-called "peripheral" cultures of Europe, based on false data, represents more than a micro-philological fallacy. A map of cultural heritage of European Enlightenment is sketched using similar micro-philological tools, and false tools produce false, misleading map. By the present state of the Locke-studies, the 18th century translations and paraphrases of his works – including his wide-spread educational writings with their different translational prefaces and notes – have an important position in the interpretation of the impact of Locke's ideas in Europe. However, the French editions, based on the translation of Pierre Costa, still figure as central ones. Ignorance of editions in Central-Europe-an languages in mainstream interpretative literature goes hand in hand with the lack of perspective on Central-European Enlightenment in the 18th century Locke-readings. As an example of those hidden Central-European Locke-readings, we shall present two characteristic cases of the Hungarian 18th century reception of Locke. Next to this example of medical perspective in interpretation of Locke's educational work, we shall also mention the 18th-century translation of Locke written by Hungarian Protestant aristocrat of Transylvania Count Ádám Székely, a follower of Voltaire. He wrote a preface to an edition he translated (Locke, 1771). Closer reading reveals the standpoint that corrupted human nature can be repaired through education done in the manner of previously mentioned Milton's "Pelagian theory". Locke's pragmatic political philosophy cannot be properly under-stood within the abovementioned denominational interpretative frame-work – therefore we should develop a new frame which could accommodate similar phenomena of the Locke-reception in Central Europe, and modestly modify the scheme of the overall European Locke-reception.

The Thoughts: Socialization and Moral Virtue

Effeminacy, morbidity and valetudinarianism are presented by Locke as the pernicious effects of physically corrupting habits acquired in youth. By forcing parents to confront their own deeply rooted prejudices about gender, Locke seeks to encourage an open minded attitude as the natural default position of parents and teachers concerned with education more generally. Inuring a child to the effects of cold and wet through habit is simply the earliest and wholly somatic practice in developing the cognitive capacity of suspending desires that grounds Locke's account of intellectual freedom in the *Essay Concerning Human Understanding* (Locke 1975). Moreover, corporal punishment contradicts the physical education directed to training endurance toward hardship. Cultivating a child's sensitivity to esteem and shame is the lynch pin of Lockean socialization. Habituation is the conceptual bridge linking the desire for esteem and rational autonomy in Locke's theory of early education. Locke presents habituation as a means to bring a child closer to the achievement of rational control over desires. Given the emphasis on experience and radical diminution of the importance of rules in Locke's account of socialization in early education, it is perhaps not surprising that Locke presents virtues as mental habits that like reading and foreign languages should be learned by children through experience rather than as academic studies. There are two prominent features of Locke's treatment of virtue. This natural "wanting more" Locke identifies as "the root of all evil". On the one hand, Locke insists that parents and teachers should never submit to imperious demands of children. Locke maintains that without this capacity to suspend desires prior to forming judgment about action, they can never have virtue. "Breeding" replaces religion as the practical foundation of virtue in Locke's proposals for early education. Locke distinguishes breeding or "civility" from virtue, for breeding is a character trait that "sets a gloss on virtues" in a social context. Parents, of course, are charged to reinforce their children's good manners assiduously. Locke's account of the qualifications and pedagogic duty of a tutor represents a kind peak in his treatment of early education. The tutor's task encompasses the full scope of Locke's new method of education with its combination of socialization and communication of ideas.

Higher Education: The Conduct

In the introduction to the *Conduct of the Understanding* Locke signals that this book on education has a different purpose and intended audience than his earlier *Thoughts*. While the argument of the *Thoughts* registered some movement from very early education through to introductory level studies of the various disciplines, Locke's focus in this work was primary and secondary education. The *Conduct*, however, is focused exclusively on higher education. The *Thoughts* and the *Conduct* are thus the root and branch of Locke's larger program of educational reform. The philosophical foundation of Locke's method in the *Conduct* is identical to that of the *Thoughts* ; namely, the relative equality of natural intellectual faculties. Locke attacks the narrow-mindedness and intellectual laziness of the English gentry and asserts that contrary to custom, reading and study is the proper business of a gentleman. The evil twin of relative equality of natural capacities is, according to Locke, the all-too-natural temperamental and intellectual defects common to human understanding. The cardinal virtue in Locke's new system of higher education is probity. It is important to recall that Locke always maintained throughout his account of early education that knowledge is distinct from habit (Neill 1989: 238). In contrast to the syllogistic reasoning characteristic of the formal logic of the universities, Locke's new method focuses on the mind's ability to control its own internal operations. In order to facilitate this practice, Locke suggests that the individual needs to adopt the Cartesian methodology of reducing every argument to "clear and distinct ideas". Much as Locke's proposals for physical education strove to make play out of necessity for children, similarly his method of higher education appeals to an individual's epistemic egoism to encourage a relish for mentally deconstructing arguments and opinions. One of the most important aims of Locke's method are to develop what he calls the practice of "bottoming." Locke's emphasis on the mind's ability through training to become conscious of, and thus capable of directing, its own activity is perhaps even more apparent in the mental activity he terms "transferring." The radical implication of Locke's argument is that complex mental activities such as bottoming and transferring are not natural intellectual gifts enjoyed by a lucky few. For Locke, the application of the method relates primarily to reading and study. In the *Conduct* Locke systematizes this call for close study of original texts and offers it as an alternative to the study of formal logic as the basis of higher education. Locke warns vociferously against the dangers of adopting opinions on the basis of sloppy, hasty, or prejudiced reading. The application of methodical reasoning to reading is the hallmark of Locke's treatment of the various studies to which the adult individual, and especially the university student, should aspire. First, Locke expands on his earlier recommendation to study mathematics in the *Thoughts*. More importantly, however, Locke sees studies in math as a way to train the mind of a scholar in following a chain of ideas and examining their connection. Locke did not mean by this that all aspects of intellectual experience can be reduced to mathematical certainty. Mathematics and close reading of texts both accustom the mind to thinking consciously about thinking clearly. Locke refers to instances of "very mean people" who have raised their minds to a "great sense and understanding of religion". Theology emerges for Locke as the democratic study *par excellence*, as a "noble study which is every man's duty" because in principle questions of salvation are every individual's concern. The egalitarian basis of Locke's method ensures that the value in close reading of texts, especially Scripture, extends to all classes.

Education and the Public

We have also seen that Locke's educational method rests on a profoundly egalitarian epistemological foundation. While Locke's novel proposals for early education are clearly developed in the context of a new understanding of the natural rights family, does his appeal to the public importance of education suggest certain limits in the family's capacity to perform a function with such vital public importance? As we have seen, Locke expressed concern about the problem of parochialism in familial-based education. Locke suggests that it is to the advantage of the family to welcome this quasi-public element into the household, especially when the tutor embodies the progressive principles of educational reform Locke advocates. McPherson and others completely miss the radical thrust of Locke's account of differential rationality. A second aspect of Locke's educational theory that most versions of the theory of possessive individualism simply do not take seriously enough is Locke's consideration of the importance of religion as a support for educational reform. The core argument of Locke's report is that the problem of poverty must be addressed through the broad application of public power to educate poor children. Corporal punishment, more or less abandoned in Locke's account of childhood education, returns with surprising éclat in his treatment of civil law. For the poor, as opposed to vagrants and beggars, Locke argues relief "consists in finding work for them". Besides the obvious advantage of dramatically expanding public access to education, Locke identifies several other benefits from this proposal. Significantly, Locke's "working schools" are not orphanages. In Locke's working school proposal we can detect the germ of a primitive public day care system. The logical outcome of the broad implementation of this proposal would be the creation of a new class of public teachers, presumably informed by Locke's novel method of education. Locke argues that this democratization of education would include boys and girls being taught together, and even allowing uneducated poor adults to attend the work schools "to learn". The effect on public morality is also a consideration for Locke.

Ideas in general and their original

All Ideas come from Sensation or Reflection. Let us then suppose the mind to be, as we say, white paper, void of all characters, without any ideas: —How comes it to be furnished? Whence comes it by that vast store which the busy and boundless fancy of man has painted on it with an almost endless variety? Whence has it all the *materials* of reason and knowledge? To this I answer, in one word, from experience. In that all our knowledge is founded; and from that it ultimately derives itself. Our observation employed either, about external sensible objects, or about the internal operations of our minds perceived and reflected on by ourselves, is that which supplies our understandings with all the *materials* of thinking. These two are the fountains of knowledge, from whence all the ideas we have, or can naturally have, do spring.

All our Ideas are of the one or the other of these.The understanding seems to me notto have the least glimmering of any ideas which it doth not receive from one of these two. *External objects* furnish the mind with the ideas of sensible qualities, which are all thosedifferent perceptions they produce in us; and *the mind* furnishes the understanding with ideas of its own operations. These, when we have taken a full survey of them, and their several modes, combinations, and relations, we shall find to contain all our whole stock of ideas; and that we have nothing in our minds which did not come in one of these two ways. Let anyone examine his own thoughts, and thoroughly search into his understanding; and then let him tell me, whether all the original ideas he has there, are any other than of the objects of his senses, or of the operations of his mind, considered as objects of his reflection. And how great a mass of knowledge soever he imagines to be lodged there, he will, upon taking a strict view, see that he has not any idea in his mind but what one of these two have imprinted;—though perhaps, with infinite variety compounded and enlarged by the understanding, as we shall see hereafter.

Idea is the Object of Thinking.Every man being conscious to himself that he thinks;and that which his mind is applied about whilst thinking being the *ideas* that are there, it is past doubt that men have in their minds several ideas, such as are those expressed by the words *whiteness, hardness, sweetness, thinking, motion, man, elephant, army, drunkenness,* andothers: it is in the first place then to be inquired, *How he comes by them?* We know it is a received doctrine, that men have native ideas, and original characters, stamped upon their minds in their very first being. This opinion I have at large examined already; and, I suppose what I have said in the foregoing Book will be much more easily admitted, when I have shown whence the understanding may get all the ideas it has; and by what ways and degrees they may come into the mind;—for which I shall appeal to everyone's own observation and experience.

Observable in Children. He that attentively considers the state of a child, at his firstcoming into the world, will have little reason to think him stored with plenty of ideas that are to be the matter of his future knowledge. Light and colours are busy at hand everywhere, when the eye is but open; sounds and some tangible qualities fail not to solicit their proper senses, and force an entrance to the mind;—but yet, I think, it will be granted easily, that if a child were kept in a place where he never saw any other but black and white till he were a man, he would have no more ideas of scarlet or green, than he that from his childhood never tasted an oyster, or a pineapple, has of those particular relishes. . . . A man begins to have ideas when he first has sensation. What sensation is.—if it shall be demanded then, when a man begins to have any ideas, I think the true answer is, —when he first has any sensation. For, since there appear not to be any ideas in the mind before the senses have conveyed any in, I conceive that ideas in the understanding are coeval with *sensation; which is such an impression or motion made in some part of the body, as produces some perception in the understanding.*

The Objects of Sensation.—First, our Senses, conversant about particular sensibleobjects, do convey into the mind several distinct perceptions of things, according to those various ways wherein those objects do affect them. And thus we come by those *ideas* we have of *yellow, white, heat, cold, soft, hard, bitter, sweet,* and all those which we call sensible qualities; which when I say the senses convey into the mind, I mean, they from external objects convey into the mind what produces there those perceptions. This great source of most of the ideas we have, depending wholly upon our senses, and derived by them to the understanding, we call sensation.

The Operations of our Minds, the other Source of them. The other fountainfrom which experience furnished the understanding with ideas is,—the perception of the operations of our own mind within us, as it is employed about the ideas it has got;—which operations, when the soul comes to reflect on and consider, do furnish the understanding, with another set of ideas, which could not be had from things without.

The Original of all our Knowledge. In time the mind comes to reflect on its own operations about the ideas got by sensation, and thereby stores itself with a new set of ideas, which we call ideas of reflection. These are the impressions that are made on our senses by outward objects that are extrinsically to the mind; and its own operations, proceeding from powers intrinsically and proper to itself, which, when reflected on by itself, become also objects of its contemplation—are, as we have said, the original of all knowledge.

Some further considerations concerning our simple ideas of sensation

Some further considerations concerning our simple ideas of sensation are as:

By motions, external, and in our organism. If then external objects be not united toour minds when they produce ideas therein; and yet we perceive these *original* qualities in such of them as singly fall under our senses, it is evident that some motion must be thence continued by our nerves, or animal spirits, by some parts of our bodies, to the brains or the seat of sensation, there to produce in our minds the particular ideas we have of them. And since the extension, figure, number, and motion of bodies of an observable bigness, may be perceived at a distance by the sight, it is evident some singly imperceptible bodies must come from them to the eyes, and thereby convey to the brain some motion; which produces these ideas which we have of them in us.

Examples. Flame is denominated hot and light; snow, white and cold; and manna,white and sweet, from the ideas they produce in us. Which qualities are commonly thought to be the same in those bodies that those ideas are in us, the one the perfect resemblance of the other, as they are in a mirror, and it would by most men be judged very extravagant if one should say otherwise? And yet he that will consider that the same fire that, at one distance produces in us the sensation of warmth, does, at a nearer approach, produce in us the far different sensation of pain, ought to bethink himself what reason he has to say—that this idea of warmth, which was produced in him by the fire, is *actually in the fire;* and his idea of pain, which the same fire produced in him the same way, is *not* in the fire. Why are whiteness and coldness in snow, and pain not, when it produces the one and the other idea in us; and can do neither, but by the bulk, figure, number, and motion of its solid parts?

How Bodies produce Ideas in us. The next thing to be considered is, how bodiesproduce ideas in us; and that is manifestly by impulse, the only way which we can conceive bodies to operate in.

How secondary Qualities produce their ideas. After the same manner that the ideasof these original qualities are produced in us, we may conceive that the ideas of *secondary* qualities are also produced, viz. by the operation of insensible particles on our senses. For, it being manifest that there are bodies and good store of bodies, each whereof are so small, that we cannot by any of our *senses* discover either their bulk, figure, or motion,—as is evident in the particles of the air and water, and others extremely smaller than those; perhaps as much smaller than the particles of air and water, as the particles of air and water are smaller than peas or hail-stones; —let us suppose at present that the different motions and figures, bulk and number, of such particles, affecting the several organs of our senses, produce in us those different sensations which we have from the colours and smells of bodies; vs. that a violet, by the impulse of such insensible particles of matter, of peculiar figures and bulks, and in different degrees and modifications of their motions, causes the ideas of the blue colour, and sweet scent of that flower to be produced in our minds.

Ideas in the Mind, Qualities in Bodies. To discover the nature of our *ideas* the better,and to discourse of them intelligibly, it will be convenient to distinguish them *as they are ideas or perceptions in our minds; and as they are modifications of matter in the bodies that cause such perceptions in us:*

that so we may not think (as perhaps usually is done) that they areexactly the images and resemblances of something inherent in the subject; most of those of sensation being in the mind no more the likeness of something existing without us, than the names that stand for them are the likeness of our ideas, which yet upon hearing they are apt to excite in us.

Ideas of primary Qualities are Resemblances; of secondary, not. From whence Ithink it easy to draw this observation,—that the ideas of primary qualities of bodies are resemblances of them, and their patterns do really exist in the bodies themselves, but the ideas produced in us by these secondary qualities have no resemblance of them at all. There is nothing like our ideas, existing in the bodies themselves. They are, in the bodies we denominate from them, only a power to produce those sensations in us: and what is sweet, blue, or warm in idea, is but the certain bulk, figure, and motion of the insensible parts, in the bodies themselves, which we call so.

Our Ideas and the Qualities of Bodies. Whatsoever the mind perceives *in itself,* or isthe immediate object of perception, thought, or understanding, that I call *idea;* and the power to produce any idea in our mind, I call *quality* of the subject wherein that power is. Thus a snowball having the power to produce in us the ideas of white, cold, and round, —the power to produce those ideas in us, as they are in the snowball, we call qualities; and as they are sensations or perceptions in our understandings, we call them ideas; which *ideas,* if we speak of sometimes as in the things themselves, we would be understood to mean those qualities in the objects which produce them in us.

Primary Qualities of Bodies. For division (which is all that a mill, or pestle, or any other body, does upon another, in reducing it to insensible parts) can never take away either solidity, extension, figure, or mobility from anybody, but only makes two or more distinct separate masses of matter, of that which was but one before; all which distinct masses, reckoned as so many distinct bodies, after division, make a certain number. These we call *original* or *primary qualities* of body, which I think we may observe to produce simple ideas inus, viz. solidity, extension, figure, motion or rest, and number.

Secondary Qualities of Bodies. Qualities which in truth are nothing inthe objects themselves but powers to produce various sensations in us by their primary qualities, i.e. by the bulk, figure, texture, and motion of their insensible parts, as colours, sounds, tastes, &c. These I call *secondary qualities.*

The ideas of the Primary alone really exist. The particular bulk, number, figure, andmotion of the parts of fire or snow are really in them,—whether anyone's senses perceive them or no: and therefore they may be called *real* qualities, because they really exist in those bodies. But light, heat, whiteness, or coldness, are no more really in them than sickness or pain is in manna. Take away the sensation of them; let not the eyes see light or colours, nor the ears hear sounds; let the palate not taste, nor the nose smell, and all colours, tastes, odours, and sounds, *as they are such particular ideas,* vanish and cease, and are reduced to their causes, i.e. bulk,figure, and motion of parts.

They depend on the primary Qualities. What we have said concerning colours andsmells may be understood also of tastes and sounds, and other the like sensible qualities; which, whatever reality we by mistake attribute to them, are in truth nothing in the objects themselves, but powers to produce various sensations in us; and depend on those primary qualities, viz. bulk, figure, texture, and motion of parts as we have said.

Conclusion: The "Essay on the Poor Law" indicates Locke's willingness to consider the use of public authority on a massive scale to combat the social ill of poverty. In this regard Locke points to what was then a whole new field of public policy. The parallel development to his call for expanded economic opportunity in a new acquisitive ethos is the possibility for expanding educational opportunity on a scale unimaginable previously in human history.This idea of employing public power to modernize, and in a sense democratize, society derived from principles of natural equality implicit in the very "bottom" of his proposals for early childhood education in the *Thoughts* and for aspiring scholars and informed citizens in the *Conduct.* The danger of replacing traditional patriarchy and political and religious authoritarianism with a new kind of state paternalism, that would concern later libertarians, may perhaps have been a risk that Locke was prepared to take, at least in the beginning of the modernization process in England. However, it is more likely that Locke anticipated the institutions of civil society would flourish with the support of his new public approach to education. The prospect of creating a society imbued at all levels with the principles of respect for the ideal of individual autonomy, cultural openness to scientific advance and critical discourse seemed in Locke's view to set a progressive course that would gradually define the nature and limits of the liberal state.

CHAPTER SEVENTEEN

CHANAKYA: A GREAT INDIAN PHILOSOPHER

Introduction

Indian literature is one of the oldest literature of the world in its broadest, sense: religious and mundane, epic lyric, prose as well as oral and written poetry and songs. Our literature has all the concept for life and its problems .Our old literary works give the meaning of life since the Vedas (3000 BC- 1000 BC) when ancient Indian literature includes only the religious classics of Hinduism, Buddhism .The great epics the Ramayana (1500BC),and the Mahabharata(1000 BC)are the, repositories of ethnic memory of the Indian peoples. But we fail to study and understand the concept of theses great works of our Rishies and Mentors. Chanakya was an ancient Indian Teacher, Philosopher, Economist, Jurist and Royal Advisor. He was Brahmin by caste approximately lived during the period 350-275 B.C. he was the son of Acharya Chanak who was a teacher. He derives his name 'Chanakya' from his father and Kautilya from his Gotra name 'Kotil' "there is less information available on Chanakya's biographical history, therefore one can rely primarily on tradition and Buddhist and Jain text of subsequent periods. Similarly Chanakya's birthplace is controversial. The Tika Hemachandra, a Jain writer, mentioned in his book 'Abhidanachintamani' Chanakya, son of Chankya was a Dramila, a resident of South India (Subramanian, 1980). Chandragupta was a brave young man belonging to a lower middle class family with no respectable position in the society on that time. Magadha or Bihar was the most powerful province in the Indian subcontinent back then but the king of Magadha Dhananand was a cruel and ruthless monarch who cared little for his subjects or the nation as a whole. When Alexander the great attacked the western part of India (Panchal) and defeated the great king of Panchal, Poras, Magadha was the only Province which has the right to challenges and stopped him. As Alexander pondered upon invading inner part of India, Chanakya, who was the teacher in the Takshshila University on that time,he visited Magadh at present Patna to request the king of Magadha Dhananand to battle Alexander's army and save the rest of India, but arrogant Dhananand refuses his proposal ,insulted and humiliated chanakya. Chanakya self respect hurt on that time and he thought to take revenge and punish and destroy Dhananand and give a capable king to Magadha. In between he decided to trained and taught Chandragupta Maurya.After long struggle he was successful in removing Dhananand and making Chandragupta Maurya as the king of Magadha Dynasty. Under the guidance of Chanakya Chandragupta become successful and established the Maurays dynasty. Now Magadha was more strong and Prosperous and Chanakya was the core of it. Chanakya was an ancient scholar who is known for his intellectual way of living life .Apart from serving as a royal advisor to king Chandragupta Maurya he has also served as a Political Science and Economics Professor of Thakshila University. According to him 'Arthashatra comprise the ethics ,the nature of government body ,market and trade ,laws of criminal court ,society and economics, most impotently 'nature of Peace' and the duties and obligation of the ruler .It is amazing that the Arthashastra also includes Mineralogy ,Agriculture ,wildlife and forest. Therefore, it covers the overall 'life' in general and relationship of human being to nature one human being to another human being (Rajeev 2). In his Chanakya Niti he gives the true lesions of life and death according to him without practicing gaining theoretical knowledge we cannot become a successful person. Chanakya has given 572 sutras in Sanskrit language .He has been a renowned scholar of Sanskrit and other Vedic Sanskrit shashtras.

Chanakya as an Educator: Chanakya was great Educator of India as well as of the world. He was Indian statesman, Great philosopher, Advisory of king and first ruler of the Mauryan Empire. He was the professor of Takhshila University. For Chanakya nothing was ever above then education .According to him 'education is the best friend and educated person is respected everywhere, 'education beats the beauty and the youth' this quote prove that knowledge was everything to him, his teaching were forever recorded in his two books namely Arthashatra and Chanakya Niti. Kautilya Arthashatra shows a very nice and accurate description of Economics, Political and Administrative problems, External invasions, making alliances with neighbouring states to keep the boarder safe. He advocated the concept of changing the department of officers from time to keep the bureaucracy corruption free .In his Arthashastra he beautifully explained that tax should not be heavy and excessive. He presented detailed outline about tax system related to tax administration, tax structure and the purpose of taxation. In other words we can say that the word 'Arthashastra' is originated from Sanskrit and it means 'Science of Politics 'or Artashasta means the economics of a society or industry is the system of organizing money and trade in it. Kautilya Arthashatra contains 15 books and with each book containing more than twenty chapters based on various topics and themes. These are the name of books in Kautilya Arthashatra: Concerning Discipline, Government Superintendents, Concerning Law, The Removal of Thorns, The Conduct of Countries, The Source of Sovereign, The End of the Six-Fold Policy, Concerning Vices and Economics, The Work of Invader, Relating to War, The Conduct of Corporation, Concerning a powerful Enemy, Strategic Means to Capture a Fortress, Secret Means and The Plan of a Treatise.

As an educator Chanakya has vast knowledge of each and every field. Each book and chapters have different subject matters like Economics, Governance, Politics, Judiciary, City Planning and even War Tactics. It is really is an all encompassing book. However, to sum up the invaluable knowledge in this ancient text, one merely needs to reads the following sutras (aphorism): Sukhsya Mulam Dharma, Dharmasya Mulam Artha, Arthasya Mulam Rajyam, Rajaysya Mulam Indrijay, Indrijay Mulam Vinayah and Vinaya Mulam Vradhopseva. It means the root of happiness is Dharma (Ethics, Righteousness), the root of dharma is Artha (Economy, Polity), the root of Artha is right governance is victorious inner-restraint, the root of humility is serving the aged. (Kautilya, Chanakya Sutra 1-6).

According to Chanakya, he insists on Indriya Vijiya /sense control for the king to attain knowledge .He insists on giving up lust, anger, greed ,vanity, arrogance, over-delight, indulgence and advises the king to cultivate intellect. Kautilya Arthashatra reminds ruler of every time, which his objectives for Duke are: Acquire Power (making present business effective); Consolidate what has been acquired (making present business effective); Expand what has been acquired (identify potential and realize it) and Enjoy what has been acquired (making it a different business for a different future). At this stage, Kautilya refers to diplomacy as an important element in Nitishastra (Foreign affairs). His clarity of thought is evident from the identification off six attributes of diplomacy. The attributes he talks about are: Intelligence, Memory, Cleverness of speech, Knowledge of politics, Morals and Readiness to provide resources.

He was the first Indian man, who introduced and advocated the idea of Constitution in India. In ancient time used to be the law as well as the judge. He has all the powers and authority. Chanakya wants to change this system first through constitution .This was a phenomenal change in Indian society as it made the ruling more systematic.

Chanakya as a Philosopher

Kautilya was a realistic and practical philosopher. His philosophy based on his experiences and situations which he faces in life .When we go through his philosophical nature we can find some moral lessons from chanakya Niti because it is a treatise on the ideal way of life and shows chanakya's deep study of the way of life. Chanakya is regarded as a great thinker and diplomat of India .He was blessed with extreme intelligence and great intellect. He has knowledge of all the field of life he also knew how to win battles and he was devious in his way. Chanakya gathered the kingdom of India together in this fight and succeeded. It is said that Chanakya was so intelligent that he had a solution to every problem that showed up. His philosophy was based on Equality for all. He give more importance for the security of the citizens was of prior most important to him. He supported agriculture for the fullest growth of the nation. In his philosophy he try to cover all phases of life as well as all emotions of human being .In each of his work he give details about the matter around him with relate the topic. He not only focus on main topic or matter but he relates all the matter with the reality of life .He has a vast knowledge of life philosophy .On that time whatever he has written it is true and most of the appropriate things in today's scenario because he had self studied, mastered and taught Gemmology (study of gemstone) Arvada, espionage (art of spying) crime, law, punishment and many more difficult subjects, for example in his Arthashastra he talk about the 'availability of water is important. It is practical to acquire a small tract of land with following water than a large tract that is dry and would need substantial investment to generate water'. His philosophy was also based on human behaviour because his human behaviour was outstanding. He advises his Swami about six emotional devils which he should avoid to all responsible human beings. He makes it amply clear that time six emotional devils do not allow appropriate decisions making in any Operations the emotions are: Kama (lust), Krodha (anger), Lobha (greed), Mana (vanity), Mada (haughtiness) and Harsh (over joy). His philosophy was based on his own inspiration and experience of life, which he presents thoroughly with the qualities and discipline. He has good subject knowledge. The real picture of Chanakya Philosophy can be seen in Chanakya Niti which is also one of the greatest work of Chanakya. His Chanakya Niti was a complete book which we also known as Chanakya Shastra or Kautilya Niti. Philosophy of Chanakya was based on realism also. He says "One should save money against hard times, and save his wife at the sacrifice of his riches but invariably one should save his soul even at the sacrifice of his wife and riches" (Davis, 2014).

Chanakya leadership Skill:

Aacharya Chanakya has excellent leadership qualities, he was also called Kautilya and Vishnugupta , was the Prime Minister in the court of Chandragupta Maurya .He was the guru of Chandragupta Maurya .and ,the Founder of Maurya Empire. It has mentioned thousand years ago that the first responsibility of a leader is to identify reality. The famous work of Chanakya is Arthashatra which is basically on the art of governance in an instructional tone. From his childhood he has excellent knowledge of leadership skills, and his level of knowledge was far beyond compare to the children of his age. He has good making power with efficient mind and action. He has great vision and was extremely wise. He was always lived by his principles his Niti and his thoughts. To make Chandragupta Maurya an emperor he had made alliances with many similar kingdoms, convinced many bigger kingdoms at that time that the Chandragupta was the most eligible person to rule Magadha and save the entire India and sub-continent from Alexander .All of this was possible only by his extensive communication skills and knowledge of statecraft and military science. The current administrative policy, Foreign policies, Military Forces in India has its origin rooted to his book Arthashatra. His aphorisms in Niti Shastra are applicable to the society in the current century as well .he uses the concept of Akahanda Bharat, at a time when India was divided into several kingdoms. His vision and thoughts were so ahead of time that it is relevant even to these days. Chanakya believed the teachers to be very powerful in society who can destroy or build empires if needed. He believed that students and teachers should stand against the government if it is corrupt or leading the anarchy. According to Chanakya Effective Communication. According to him 'a good leader does not stop until the task at his hand is finished.He rests only after he finishes his work. He is not afraid of failure.

Chanakya said people who work sincerely are the happiest. Most people fail because they just do not carry on.'These qualities should improve the leadership skills: Positive Attitude, Effective Communication, Decision Making, Happiness, Accountability, Punctuality, Maintain Secrecy, Devotion and Healthy Behaviour. So we can say that chanakya has good leadership qualities, that's why he was the chief adviser of two Mauryan Emperors and was one of finest brains the country has ever had.

Chanakya Quotes-"When in the court, he shall never cause his petitioners to wait at the door, for when a king makes himself inaccessible to his people and entrusts his work to his immediate officers, he may be sure to engender confusion in business and to cause there by Public disaffection, an himself a prey to his enemies."

According to Chanakya, Leaders need to understand that sending people to a communication skills workshop does not improve communication in the organization, communication improves when the channels of communication are kept open the channels of communication are kept both vertically and horizontically.

He was decision Making man he talks about decisions in his Niti Shastra: before you start work, always ask yourself three questions: why I am doing it, what the result might be and will be successful. Only when you think deeply and find satisfactory answers to these questions go ahead.

"Consider again and again the following: the right time, the right friends, the right place, the right means of income, the right ways of spending, and from whom you derive your power.

Chanakya Quotes "All urgent calls he shall hear at once, but never put off; for when postponed, they will prove too hard or impossible to accomplish." he says a good and efficient leader should never postpone decisions and should make fast and effective decisions.

According to him in an organization employ can be happy according to their need completion.

He Quotes: "in the happiness of his subject lies his happiness ;in their welfare ;whatever pleases himself he shall not consider as good, but whatever pleasures his subjects he shall consider as good.

According to Chanakya, a good leader realizes that his/her whims and preferences come secondary to the real needs and issues of the organization.

In his leadership rules he says that "An egoist can be won over by being respected, a crazy person can be won over by allowing him to behave in an insane manner and a wise person can be won over by truth".

Conclusion: Kautilya, Vishnugupta or Chanakya all names gives meaning to our education system in our politics, management even philosophy of Dharma, Karma, Kaama, Moksha and our vision and mission of present scenario. He was great men, good teacher, good adviser, good philosophy; he was greatest Indian diplomat of all time. He has given notable contribution to our society and the world. This is just a brief introduction to Chanakya Niti and Chanakya Arthashsatra .In contemporary world if our rulers follow Chanakya Niti, then the country would definitely prosper and strong impregnable vibrant nation emerges .Therefore Chanakya Niti is relevant even today and will be future also .Something definitely not flitted in present society but whatever we can gain and accept from Chanakya works it will de definitely beneficial for us and for the nation also. There are many teaching and lesions of Chankaya holding meaning and beauty even today. I agree that it is really hard to follow his teaching methodology in present society, but it makes a difference once you follow Chanakya ideologies. We cannot judge all his philosophies in this present scenario because he told some good and may be some bad. Just to try to grasp all good things and leave which in not applicable in present prospective.

Bibliography

Aarsleff, Hans. (1994). "Locke's influence." In *The Cambridge Companion to Locke*, edited by Vere Chappell, 252-89. Cambridge, England: Cambridge University Press.

Ashcraft, Richard (1969). "John Locke's Library. Portrait of an Intellectual", *Trans-actions of the Cambridge Bibliographical Society*, Vol. 5, No. 1, pp. 47–60.

Brady, Michelle. (2005). "The Nature of Virtue in a Politics of Consent: John Locke on Education." *International Philosophical Quarterly* Vol. 45, No. 2 [June]: 157-73.

Brown, Andrew F. (1952), "On Education: John Locke, Christian Wolff and the 'Moral Weeklies'", *University of California Publications in Modern Philo logy*, Vol. 36, No. 5, pp. 149–172.

Carrig, Jopseph. (2001). "Liberal Impediments to Liberal Education: The Assent to Locke." *Review of Politics* Vol. 63, No. 1 (Winter): 41-76.

Dunn, John (1969), *The Political Thought of John Locke: A Historical Account of the Argument of the "Two Treatises of Government"*, Cambridge: CambridgeUniversity Press.

Dunn, John (1984), *Locke,* Oxford/New York: Oxford University Press.

Ezzel, Margaret (1991), "John Locke's Images of Childhood", in: Richard Ashcraft (ed.), *John Locke. Critical Assessments*, London/New York: Routledge, Vol. 2, pp. 231–245.

Filmer, Robert. (1991). "Patriarcha" in *Patriarcha and Other Writings.* Johann P. Somerville, ed. Cambridge: Cambridge University Press.

Forde, Steven. (2006). "What does Locke Expect Us to Know?" *Review of Politics.* Vol. 68, No. 1 (Winter): 232-58.

Gauthier, David (1977), "Why Ought One Obey God? Reflections on Hobbes and Locke", *Canadian Journal of Philosophy*, Vol. 7, No. 3, pp. 429–443.

Lock, János [Locke, John] (1771/1829), *A' gyermekek' neveléséről* [*On the Educa-tion of Children*], Kolo'sváratt: Reform. Coll.; 2nd edition, Buda: Burián Pál.

Locke, John (1968), *The Educational Writings*, James L. Axtell (ed.), Cambridge: Cambridge University Press.

Locke, John (2007), *The Reasonableness of Christianity as Delivered in the Scrip-tures*, John J. Higgins-Biddle (ed.), Oxford: Clarendon Press.

Locke, John (2008), *A Paraphrase and Notes on the Epistles of St. Paul to the Galatians, 1 and 2 Corinthians, Romans, Ephesians*, Arthur W. Wainwright(ed.), Oxford: Clarendon Press.

Marshall, John (1994), *Resistance, Religion and Responsibility*, Cambridge: Cam-bridge University Press.

McLachlan, Herbert (1976), *The Religious Opinions of Milton, Locke and Newton*, Manchester: Norwood Editions.

Milton, John (1991), *John Milton*, Stephen Orgel, Jonathan Goldberg (eds.), Ox-ford/New York: Oxford University Press.

Neill, Alex (1991), "Locke on Habituation, Autonomy, and Education", in: Ri-chard Ashcraft (ed.), *John Locke. Critical Assessments*, London/New York: Routledge, Vol. 2, pp. 246–265.

Neill, Alex. 1989. "Locke on Habituation, Autonomy, and Education." *Journal of the History of Philosophy* Vol. 27, No. 2 (April): 225-45.

Spellman, W.M. (1988), *John Locke and the Problem of Depravity*, Oxford: Ox-ford University Press.

Spellman, W.M. (1991), "The Christian Estimate of Man in Locke's Essay", in: Richard Ashcraft (ed.), *John Locke. Critical Assessments*, London/ New York: Routledge, Vol. 2, pp. 191–227.

Tarcov, Nathan. 1984. *Locke's Education for Liberty*. Chicago: University of Chicago Press.

Walker, Caren M. and Alison Gopnik. "Toddlers Infer Higher-Order Relational Principles in Causal Learning." *Psychological Science* 25 (2014): 161-169.

Weszprémi, István (1760), *A' kisded gyermekeknek nevelésekröl való rövid oktatás* [*A Short Teaching about the Education in Early Childhood*], Kolo'sváratt: Páldi István.

Yolton, John W. (ed.) (1969), *John Locke: Problems and Perspectives. A Collection of New Essays*, Cambridge: Cambridge University Press.

Kalam, APJ Abdul. Ignited Minds: Penguin Books Ltd., 2002.

Kalam APJ Abdul. Wings of Fire: Universities Press India Private Limited, 1999.

Anirban,1998 Exploring Student Politics, Published by Manasi Banerjee.

Poddar, Aurobindo 1976 'Introduction' to Isvar Chandra Vidyasagara 1976 Marriage of Hindu Widows, K.P.Bagchi & Company, Calcutta.

Ray, Binoy Bhushan,2011 'Sikshasar ' theke 'Barnaparichay'-Samajer sange prathamikl pather bibartan' Chikibhusan Prakashani, Kolkata .

Mrunalini,T. 2020. *Philosophical Foundation Of Education*. India. Neelkamal Publication.

Arulsamy, S. 2018. *Philosophical And Sociological Perspective of education*. India. Neelkamal Publication.

Swaroop, S. 2009. *Philosophical and sociological foundation of education*. Vinay Rajkheja Publishers.

Bhatia,K. *Theory and principles of education*. Doaba house.

Arulsamy,S. 2018. *Philosophical And Sociological Perspective of education*. India.Neelkamal Publication.

Mrunalini,T. 2020. *Philosophical Foundation Of Education*. India. Neelkamal Publication.

N.R. Sawroop Saxena,(2013). Philosophical and Sociology Foundation of Education- Pub

by Vinay Rakkeja, C/O R.Lall Book Depot. Page No: 250-256.

Daud, W. (1998). *Educational Philosophy and Practice of Syed Muhammad Naquib Al-Attas: An Exposition of the Original Concept of Islamization*. Kuala Lumpur: International Institute of Islamic Thoughts and Civilization.

Gupta, K. S. (2005). *The Philosophy of Rabindranath Tagore*. Aldeshot Hemisphere: Ashgate

Jha, N. (1999). "Rabindranath Tagore", PROSPECTS The Quarterly Journal of Education. Paris: UNESCO National Bureau of Education

Kumar, R. (2008). 'India as a Foreign Policy Actor – Normative Redux', Centre for European Policy Studies

Kumar, R. (2008)"Rabindranath Tagore: Complete Personality". Department of History, Meerut College.

Palmer, J. A. (ed.) (2001). *Fifty Key Thinkers on the Environment*. New York: Routledge

Sharma, R. (2002). *Textbook of Educational Philosophy*. New Delhi: Kanishka Publishers.p.320

Tagore, R. (1961). *Towards Universal Man*. New York: Asia Publishing House.

Tagore, R. (1917). *My Reminiscences*. New York: The Macmillan Company.

Tagore, R. (1929). *Ideals of Education*, The Visva-Bharati Quarterly (April-July), pp.73-74

Sarkar, P. R., Discourses on Prout, *The Electronic Edition of the Works of P.R. Sarkar, Version 7.0, Ananda Marga Publication, Calcutta,* 1959.

Anandamitra, The spiritual philosophy of shrii shrii Anandamurti: Commentary on Ananda Sutram(2nd Edition), Ananda Marga Publications, Denver, 1998.

Towsey, Michel, Eternal Dance of Macrocosm An Encyclopedia of Matter, Mind, and Consciousness, vol-2, 2011.

Eddington, Arthur, The Nature of the Physical World, Macmillan Company, New York, 1928.

Mookerji, Ajit, Tantra Asana-A Way of Self-Realization, published by Ravi Kumar, p. 62, 1965,

Vivekananda Rachana Samagra, Editor; Prasun Basu, Sachindranath Bhattachrya,Vabapatra Publication, 1993

Chintanayak Vivekananda, Editor: Swami Lokeshwarananda, Rakrishna Mission Institute Of Culture, Golpark, 2004

Singh, Y.K. Philosophical Foundation of Education, New Delhi: APH Publishing Corporation, 2007,

Johri, Pradeep Kumar, Educational Thought, New Delhi: Anmol Publications PVT. LTD., 2005,

Pani, S.P. and Pattnaik, S.K. Vivekananda, Aurobindo and Gandhi on Education, New Delhi: Anmol Publications PVT. LTD., 2006

Swami Sarvabhutananda (1993), *My India, the Eternal India,* Ramakrishna Mission Institute of Culture, Kolkata, India

Ravi.S.Samuel. (2011), 'A *Comprehensive study of Education,*' PHI Learning Private Limited, New Delhi, 110001.

Banerjee, A. (2020). Ethics and Human Evolution: A Perspective from Sri Aurobindo. The Philosophy of Sri Aurobindo: Indian Philosophy and Yoga in the Contemporary World, 153.

Banerji, D. (2020). Sri Aurobindo, Enlightenment, and the Bengal Renaissance: A Discourse on Evolution of Consciousness. The Philosophy of Sri Aurobindo: Indian Philosophy and Yoga in the Contemporary World, 33.

Bhattacharjee, I. (2020). Rabindranath Tagore and the Question of the Teacher's Vocation. David Hansen and the Call to Teach: Renewing the Work That Teachers Do, 119.

Cardozo, E. (2021). 'The Sagacity of Words': Gandhi and 21st century hip-hop. Exchanges: The Interdisciplinary Research Journal, 8(3), 1-12.

Dash, B. M., & Nagar, A. (2020). Relevance of Hinduism in social work. In Indian Social Work (pp. 165-172). Routledge India.

Gajare, J. P. (2020). Raising Need of Organizational Behavior Modification in Business Organizations with Reference to Chanakya's Yogic Approach of Business Management.

Gandhi, M. K. (2020). Religious Pacifism. Works Righteousness: Material Practice in Ethical Theory, 109.

Hartz, R. (2021). Spiritual pragmatism: William James, Sri Aurobindo and global philosophy. In Pragmatism, Spirituality and Society (pp. 221-246). Palgrave Macmillan, Singapore.

Jahn, E. (2021). The National and Universal Importance of the Non-violent Policy of Mohandas K. Gandhi. In Decolonising Conflicts, Security, Peace, Gender, Environment and Development in the Anthropocene (pp. 245-277). Springer, Cham.

Medhananda, S. (2020). Was Swami Vivekananda a Hindu Supremacist? Revisiting a Long-Standing Debate. Religions, 11(7), 368.

Mukherjee, H. B. (2020). Education for fullness: A study of the educational thought and experiment of Rabindranath Tagore. Taylor & Francis.

Namani, M., Khanjarkhani, M., & Davarpanah, A. (2020). Study of the viewpoint of Rabindranath Tagore and his educational implications. Journal of Subcontinent Researches, 12(39), 243-262.

Parikh, M. (2020). Leadership lessons from Shukraniti: a post-Vedic perspective. International Journal of Indian Culture and Business Management, 21(3), 410-434.

Ramya, C. (2020). Sri Aurobindo as 'The Pioneer of the New Age and the Spokesman of the New Truth': An Appraisal. International Journal on Multicultural Literature, 10.

Rath, A., & Sharma, S. (2021). Sarvepalli Radhakrishnan. Studies in Humanities and Social Sciences, 26(1), 151-171p.

Sarkar, T. Comparison between the Educational thoughts of Rabindranath Tagore and Mahatma Gandhi. Journal homepage: www. ijrpr. com ISSN, 2582, 7421.

Sharma, M. K., & Sharma, R. C. (2021). Innovation Framework for Excellence in Higher Education Institutions. Global Journal of Flexible Systems Management, 22(2), 141-155.

Sharma, N. (2021). From Buddha to Tagore and Gandhi: Value-Creating Curricula in India. In Oxford Research Encyclopedia of Education.

Talukdar, D. (2020). Swami Vivekananda" s Life And Philosophy. European Journal of Molecular & Clinical Medicine, 7(5), 193-196.

Van Niekerk, B. (2020). Swami Vivekananda: Revival and reform in the making of Hinduism. HTS Theological Studies, 76, 1-8.

Basham, AL. (1989). The Origins and Development of Classical Hinduism, Boston: Beacon Press.

Chatterjee, S.G. and Dutta, D.M. (1960). An Introduction to Indian Philosophy. Calcutta: University of Calcutta Press.

Everett, C. C. (1899). "The Psychology of the Vedanta and Sankhya Philosophies". Journal of the American Oriental Society, 20, 309-316.

Hiriyanna, M. (1932). The Essentials of Indian Philosophy. London: George Allen and Unwin Press.

Hiriyanna, M. (1993). Outlines of Indian Philosophy. First Indian Edition. New Delhi, India: Motilal Banarsidass Publishers Private Limited.

Keith, A.B. (1918). The Samkhya System. Oxford: Clarendon Press.

Majumdar, A.K. (1926b) "The Personalistic Conception of Nature as Expounded in the Sankhya Philosophy". The Philosophical Review, 35 (1), 53-63.

Radhakrishnan, S. (1977). Indian Philosophy, Volume 2. Tenth Impression. London: George Allen & Unwin.

Ranganathananda, Swami. (19800. The Message of the Upanishads. Bombay, India: Bharti ya Vidya Bhavan. Shrimad Bhagvadgita,. Gorakhpur, India: Gita Press.

Schweizer, P. (1993). "Mind/Consciousness Dualism in Sankhya-Yoga Philosophy". Philosophy and Phenomenological Research, 53 (4), 845-859.

Taimni, I.K. (1961). The Science of Yoga. A commentary on The Yoga Sutras of Patanjali. Wheaton, IL: The Theosophical Publishing House.

Doyle, James, F., ed. (1973). Educational Judgments: Papers in the Philosophy of Education. London: Routledge & Kegan Paul.

Gupta, S. (2005). Education in Emerging India. Teachers role in Society. New Delhi, Shipra Publication.

Leaman, Oliver, ed. (1998). The Future of Philosophy towards the 21st Century. London and New York: Routledge.

Clabaugh, G. K. & Rozycki, E. G. (1996), Foundation of Education and the Devaluation of Teacher Preparation. In F. B. Murray (Ed.), The Teacher Educator's Handbook: Building a Knowledge Base or the Preparation of Teachers. San Francisco, Jossey – Bass.

Council of Learned Societies in Education (1986), Standards for Academic and Professional Instruction in Foundations of Education, Educational Studies, and Educational Policy Studies. Ann Arbor, MI Praken.

Cremin, L. A. (1961), The Transformation of the School: Progressivism in American Education, 1867-1957, New York, Knopf.

Cuban, L. (1984), How Teachers Taught: Consistency and Change in American Classrooms 1890-1980, New York, Langman.

www.ingramcontent.com/pod-product-compliance
Lightning Source LLC
Chambersburg PA
CBHW071421150726

48000CB00001B/427